Edna Ferber's America

EDNA FERBER'S
AMERICA

Eliza McGraw

Louisiana State University Press
Baton Rouge

Published by Louisiana State University Press
Copyright © 2013 by Louisiana State University Press
All rights reserved
Manufactured in the United States of America
First printing

DESIGNER: Michelle A. Neustrom
TYPEFACE: Whitman
PRINTER AND BINDER: Maple Press

LIBRARY OF CONGRESS CATALOGING-IN-PUBLICATION DATA

McGraw, Eliza R. L.
   Edna Ferber's America / Eliza McGraw.
      pages cm
   Includes bibliographical references and index.
   ISBN 978-0-8071-5188-4 (cloth : alk. paper) — ISBN 978-0-8071-5189-1
(pdf) — ISBN 978-0-8071-5190-7 (epub) — ISBN 978-0-8071-5191-4 (mobi)
1. Ferber, Edna, 1887–1968—Criticism and interpretation. I. Title.
   PS3511.E46Z75 2013
   813'.52—dc23

                                                           2013005785

The paper in this book meets the guidelines for permanence and durability
of the Committee on Production Guidelines for Book Longevity
of the Council on Library Resources. ∞

For my mother, Rosemarie Russi Howe

Contents

Acknowledgments

Writing *Edna Ferber's America* has been a very long process, and I truly appreciate all of the help I received along the way.

Cassie Young undertook much of the archival research and sent me sheaves of Ferber correspondence and materials from archives I couldn't visit. She read pages and pages of Ferber material and found many things I wouldn't have otherwise seen.

The outside reader from LSU Press read many versions and offered keen insight and suggestions. John Easterly first saw the promise in this project, and Margaret Lovecraft has spent much time and effort in completing the book. Stan Ivester had the unenviable task of copyediting, and his work made my writing much clearer.

Gary Richards and Alison Piepmeier, just as they did when we were all in graduate school, have borne the brunt of my writing so much of this book with no other English professors around. They have read, discussed, and most importantly, listened.

Eric Felten explained what Edna Ferber drank at the Algonquin Round Table (a horse's neck) and was consistently enthusiastic about my topic.

My family and friends supported my work through the long period of research, reading, and writing. Adam, Simon, and Macie offered in-house support, company, and patience with my Edna Ferber preoccupation.

This book is dedicated to my mother, Rosemarie R. Howe, because she is a Ferber aficionado from way back, and she never confuses the movies with the novels.

Edna Ferber's America

INTRODUCTION

WHENEVER I'M ASKED WHO EDNA FERBER WAS, I often find the quickest way to identify her is to say, "She wrote *Giant*," or "She wrote *Show Boat*"; I only name her novels that have been made into famous movies or adapted for the stage. This conversational shortcut, however, presents its own problem: many people remember James Dean slouching through the film version of *Giant*, or the opening bars of "Ol' Man River" from the musical *Show Boat* rather than Ferber's books themselves.

If Ferber were anywhere near as famous today as she was in her own time, readers would never ask who she was. Her Pulitzer-winning novel *So Big* sold three million copies in 1924, and there were eight movies made of her books. Ferber was one of the highest-paid authors at Doubleday. She lunched at the Algonquin Round Table with Dorothy Parker and Alexander Woollcott. Booksellers bought almost 100,000 copies in advance of her novel *Giant*'s 1952 publication. She was a full-fledged literary celebrity and a respected chronicler of America, ranging across the country for historic moments ripe for her own personal brand of depiction. She wrote about the statehood campaigns of Alaska and Oklahoma, showboat culture on the Mississippi River, the horse racing and spa season at Saratoga, and how oil was changing Texas. Her characters include a white midwestern lumber baron, a multiracial Alaskan stateswoman, a Jewish peddler traipsing the late-nineteenth-century West, Polish immigrants farming New England, and a Creole woman who storms Saratoga Springs. With these varied figures, Ferber focused broadly on individuals shaping their own regions and lives, but kept America—her most important character—at the center of each novel.

1

Edna Ferber was born in Kalamazoo, Michigan, in 1885. Her father Jacob was from Hungary, and her mother Julia was a second-generation German immigrant. The young Jewish family kept stores, first in Ottumwa, Iowa, where anti-Semites attacked them. "My other cheek was all worn out long before I grew up," Ferber wrote of those years, which formed a background for her novelistic preoccupations and thematic concerns with ethnicity and cultural categorization (Gilbert 1978, 432). As Eileen Watts writes, "[o]ne suspects that Ferber's career was her way of proving that 'the little Jew girl' was, indeed, an acceptable American" (2007, 42). In other words, negotiating identity terms—Jew, female, American—was a personal as well as a literary preoccupation of Ferber's.

When Edna was twelve, the Ferbers moved to Appleton, Wisconsin, a more welcoming town with a larger Jewish community. The dry-goods business kept the family afloat, but Jacob's poor health left Julia to run the store alone. Through her childhood, Ferber read rapaciously, preferring Charles Dickens's work. Her hard-pressed family always found time and money to attend plays, Ferber remembered, and she established a lifetime appreciation for the theater, a theme that persists through her novels. She dreamed of becoming an actress, but as a teenager, Ferber found herself tending to her increasingly ill father, working in the family store, and writing for the Appleton *Daily Crescent*. At eighteen, she moved to Milwaukee and wrote for the *Journal,* sending money home and finding her own education at the newspaper. Whether reading or writing, Ferber made sense of her cultural moment through literary frameworks.

Jacob Ferber died in 1909, and in 1910 Edna suffered a physical breakdown and moved to Chicago, where her mother and sister had relocated. Her first novel, the 1911 *Dawn O'Hara,* draws on these experiences. She began selling her short stories to magazines such as *The Cosmopolitan* and *American Magazine*, mainly her stories featuring Emma McChesney, a white traveling saleswoman who epitomized the stereotype-breaking strong woman character that Ferber became famous for depicting and embodied herself. She wanted to go to France during World War I, but was denied a passport because of her Hungarian-born father. By 1920 she was dividing her time between New York and her mother's place in Chicago.

In 1921, Ferber's *The Girls* was serialized in *Woman's Home Companion,* which brought her fame as a novelist along with as a short-story writer and celebrity. Reporters wrote colorful portraits about her. "There is a vitality about Edna Ferber that is recognizable the moment she comes into a room," Rogers Dickinson wrote in a 1925 monograph called *Edna Ferber: A Sketch* (7). "She enters almost in a rush, with a quick, firm step; though she is short, scarcely more than five foot three, I should think, she dominates most groups" (7). By the late 1920s Ferber was ensconced as a regular fixture at the Algonquin Round Table, lunching with New York cognoscenti such as Woollcott, Walter Lippmann, and Jerome Kern. There she traded barbs, calling a harsh reviewer "as whimsical as a bowl of oatmeal" (Gilbert 1978, 181). Ferber won the Pulitzer Prize in 1925 for her novel *So Big*, which detailed the arduous life of a Chicago girl who marries a poor farmer. She collaborated with George Kaufman, another Round Table member, on plays such as *Stage Door* (1926) and *Dinner at Eight* (1932). Publishing wheels spun fast as soon as she wrote a new book; for example, the novel *Show Boat* was published in 1926, and the musical version was on Broadway in 1927.

Ferber wrote the novels *Cimarron* (1929), *American Beauty* (1939), and *Come and Get It* (1935) within six years. She took a bit of a break to write *A Peculiar Treasure*, her first autobiography, in 1939, and then returned to fiction with *Saratoga Trunk* (1941), *Great Son* (1945) *Giant* (1952), and *Ice Palace* (1958). The books were bestsellers and caused controversies as well. When *Cimarron* angered the Oklahomans it was based upon, and *Giant* did the same to Texans, Ferber waved off the provincial criticism—and sold books. "She is an old hand at having whole sections of the country wailing in anguish," wrote Lewis Nichols in *The New York Times Book Review* (1952, 30).

Ferber never married, and rumors of love affairs remained rumors. Her mother was a consistent force in her life, and Ferber financially supported both Julia and her sister, Fannie. She spent some time in the country at Treasure Hill, her rural Connecticut home, but eventually sold it and spent her last years based in New York, still traveling occasionally to do research for a novel about American Indians, which she never finished. Ferber died of stomach cancer at home in 1968. She was eighty-two years old.

Ferber's literary legacy has typically been seen as her portraits of authoritative female characters. When academics, in particular, turn to Ferber's novels, it is often to note her depictions of strong women in positions of power. As Ann Shapiro writes, "Ferber's literary trademark became heroic sagas, usually of women battling the odds in a man's world—a triumph her own career seemed to signify" (2002, 52). Ferber's work first gained this powerful-woman reputation with Emma McChesney, the traveling saleslady who took on a male-dominated business world with success, even while longing for a more domestic life. The vigor of McChesney and other characters like her are often attributed to the influence of Ferber's mother. And, of course, Ferber herself lived the example of a strong, professional woman who succeeded in the male-dominated world of American publishing.

Critics have long considered Ferber's writing "middlebrow," defined in Lisa Botshon and Meredith Goldsmith's *Middlebrow Moderns* as "[n]ot quite 'vulgar' and real enough to be deemed low culture, nor sophisticated or experimental enough for high culture" (2003, 3). More notably, as they write, "Neither 'high' literary producers nor 'low' dime-store novel creators, [these] women writers . . . succeeded in the marketplace: published by major presses, they made bestseller lists and bridged gaps in an audience increasingly fragmented by economic, racial, ethnic, and regional differences" (2003, 6). Ferber herself never understood why a large audience made her less literary. "What's wrong with writing a book that lots of people buy?" she asked ("Ferber Fundamentals" 1945).

Ferber aptly fits this category of widely read female authors along with contemporaries such as Fannie Hurst, Zona Gale, and Dorothy Canfield Fisher, all of whom wrote books in which contemporary gender roles were manipulated and often challenged. Hurst, in particular, aligns with Ferber as she employed some of the same themes of ethnic anxiety, including Jewishness in the 1930 *Back Street* and "passing" for white in the 1933 *Imitation of Life*.

What Goldsmith and Botshon call an "increasingly fragmented" audience consumed Ferber's work about its increasingly fragmented society. They found that her novels addressed the separate categories of American life—from race to ethnicity, class to religion—in a way that acknowledged distinctions, but also formed an organic portrait of an ever-changing nation. As contemporary critic Frederic Van De Water wrote: "There are things equally precious and alluring to be found in even the drabbest stretches of this nation's terrain if you know where to look and how. Most people—even most writers—don't, but Miss Ferber does" (1931, 7). Her perceived knowledge of the American scene, even though her depictions were often far from precious or alluring, encouraged people to read her books as well as accept them as one writer's chronicles of the country.

That wide readership alone places her firmly in the "middlebrow" category, but for Ferber's work, the concept of the middlebrow does not represent just a genre. It also forms a site at which literature can create category-destroying connections and enable a broader and more complex vision of America. Her middlebrow-ness represented a wider range of interpretations within her novels and readers on the outside. Ferber's work was taken in by large swaths of readers, and its intersectionality—her multilayered depictions of continuously evolving class and gender roles—fed its wide applicability.

Indeed, Ferber's writing straddled and surmounted such lines for at least one frankly highbrow contemporary reader. Harlem Renaissance poet Langston Hughes told an interviewer that "Edna Ferber originally wrote stories of Jewish life, but she broadened her perspective and went on to write *So Big, Show Boat* and *Cimarron*. I think we [African American writers] are headed in the direction of similar and perhaps superior achievement" (1950, 311). (Hughes must have been referring to *Fanny Herself,* Ferber's autobiographically informed early novel with his comment about her "stories of Jewish life"). But the idea that an accomplished and "high" writer like Hughes read and looked toward Ferber, even while acknowledging that he hoped for "perhaps superior achievement," from fellow African American writers, indicates her ability to transcend genre, to appeal both to higher literary minds as well as people looking for a good story.

Given all this contemporary appeal, why don't many readers, regardless of brow height, pick up Ferber's novels today? A recent paperback reprint of *So Big,* for example, sold around seven thousand copies. There are various reasons for the elision. For one, Ferber's novels feature unwieldy plots. It is easy to see that, as she mentions in her autobiographies, Ferber adored the writing of Charles Dickens. Her narratives sprawl similarly to those of *Bleak House* or *David Copperfield,* over time, place, and topic. Dickensian deprivations, coincidences, and transformations form a building block of Ferber's novels. And because multidynastic families are key components of much of Ferber's work, many characters have the same or similar names, often adding a layer of confusion on a first read.

Ferber herself was conscious that her writing was not always self-explanatory for all readers. "They [the novels] were all about people and fundamental things, not written in the style of the day for the people of a particular day. Behind all the things I have written there has been something I really wanted to say," she told the *New York Times* in 1952 (Nichols 1952, 30). The thorniness of Ferber's plots often appropriately mirrors the topics they cover, some of which provoke anxiety or display opacity.

The vastness and intertwined nature of these plots can seem wearisome, and was remarked upon even in Ferber's heyday. "[Ferber] is frequently illogical, free in her use of coincidence," wrote an anonymous *New York Times* reviewer in 1930 ("Miss Ferber's Vivid Tale" 1930, 3). Yet even that curmudgeonly reviewer admitted that Ferber's writing was well worth the tangled plots: "Read it for its vivid re-creation of the scenes through which Yancey and Sabra [*Cimarron* characters] lived, for its splendidly kaleidoscopic view of a young American city coming into existence, with its shifting social patterns and its broad diversity of types" (3). Today as in 1930, Ferber's work provides a "splendid kaleidoscope" that demands our attention as she uses the extensive reach of her novels to underscore the vastness of America and its concerns.

As Ferber's novels were converted into plays and movies, these turbulent plots were necessarily streamlined. Also, because Ferber was an intelligent negotiator who arranged for her novels to appear first as serials, released them, and then sold them to Hollywood, it is easy only to think of her works in conjunction with their more famous onscreen versions. J. E. Smyth explains how essential these versions were to the audiences of their time: "Ferber . . . projected a hybrid historical vision that challenged proscribed boundaries between high and low culture, history, fiction, and cinema, and gender, race, and power" (2010, 5). This sweeping ability to transcend in-place taxonomy—confronting categories, and often refuting them—is a hallmark of Ferber's, in any iteration of her vision.

It is important to remember, however, that this complicated and crucial "historical vision," including its complicated plots, began on the printed page. *Edna Ferber's America* deals closely with twelve of these works, all novels, beginning with the 1921 *Dawn O'Hara* and ending with the 1958 *Ice Palace*. I do not discuss the Emma McChesney books—*Roast Beef Medium* (1913), *Personality Plus* (1914), and *Emma McChesney and Co.* (1915) at any length, but focus instead on what are typically called the "regional novels"—*So Big* (1924), *Show Boat* (1926), *Cimarron* (1929), *American Beauty* (1931), *Come and Get It* (1935), *Saratoga Trunk* (1941), *Great Son* (1945), *Giant* (1952), and *Ice Palace* (1958)—as well as three earlier novels: *Dawn O'Hara* (1911), *Fanny Herself* (1917), and *The Girls* (1921). Although these three are not usually included in the list of regional novels, these texts initiate the themes of ethnicity that I further examine in the later works.

Images from the films have become intertwined with those from the books over the years, which happened both because the films' plots often cleave close to those of the novels and because of Ferber's cinema-conscious business sense. More crucially, Ferber's novels—the earlier ones in particular—include outmoded and racist language and depictions even as they explore complex ethnic issues. All the movies, of course, do not successfully elide racism—for example, some of the onscreen African American characters in the film version of *Show Boat* fulfill damaging stereotypes—but the books probably provide more distasteful material. As Mollie Wilson writes, "Today these novels seem dated, partly because of their author's vaudeville-era tolerance for ethnic stereotypes; but cringe-worthy caricatures . . . exist alongside some very thoughtful explorations of American racism. . . . [A]s her stories found new life in the medium of film, her books stayed stubbornly rooted in their own time" (2007). And as Carol Batker writes in an essay grouping Ferber with contemporary authors Fannie Hurst and Anna Yezierska, "The grossly racialized stereotypes of African Americans in Ferber and Hurst's fiction (and of American Indians elsewhere in Ferber's texts) can be seen as a strategic embrace of racism. Positioning themselves as white and embracing a social mobility denied to non-whites, they used settlement rhetoric to argue for Jewish integration and to deflect anti-Semitism" ("Literary Reformers" 2000, 98). As Batker writes, the use of these stereotypes is troubling because of its inherent racism, and is further complicated by Ferber's own status as Jewish, an ethnic status often figured—like that of mixed-race individuals—as straddling the color line in America, and that same status that Watts and Ferber herself point to as a motivating factor in her writing.

When read while taking this anxiety into account, Ferber's literary navigation of ethnicity issues provides some of the most salient and compelling portions of her work. Rather than ignore the novels in favor of the films, readers should examine Ferber's writing in its novelistic—if sometimes challenging— form. Especially within the earlier novels, ethnic stereotypes and slurs are patently unpleasant. Yet their existence within Ferber's charged striving to portray the similarly electric society she drew renders the whole worthwhile of further study and time, because the tensions reveal her understanding of the complicated cultural moments she chooses to portray. "She carefully wrote outsiders as observers into most of her novels," writes Donna Campbell, "all the while positing a deep complicity and sense of identification between herself and America" (2003, 26).

Ferber takes on issues of race, class, and gender, foregrounding issues such as passing, ethnic mixture, and social mobility. Read in conjunction with her own rehearsal of some of her era's tired ethnic saws, Ferber's use, exploration, and sometimes explosion of those stereotypes add intriguing points of pressure. Her novels' takes on ethnicity and class explode any social dicta set before her characters, from Mexican people in Texas to Polish people in New England to African American people along the Mississippi River. Mixture of long-entrenched white American families with those of Mexican, Aleut, and recent immigrant status (although Ferber is quick to point out that all "Americans" were immigrants at one point) is a key to financial and social success in her novels.

Ethnicity is, of course, a popular and multivalent word in today's literary lexicon, and while Ferber's work can be used effectively to put pressure upon current questions of identity politics in American literature, one way into a discussion of the ethnicity issues that surround Ferber's works is with a more contemporary reading. In 1916, when Ferber was still in full McChesney mode, philosopher John Dewey wrote, "The fact is the genuine American, the typical American, is himself a hyphenated character. . . . He is not American plus Pole or German. But the American is himself Pole-German-English-French-Spanish-Italian-Greek-Irish-Scandinavian-Bohemian-Jew and so on. The point is to see to it that the hyphen connects instead of separates" (1916, 205). Dewey's essay concerns public education, but Ferber's novels are concerned with those very hyphens in her novels. The connection may be uneasy or fraught, but by tackling the identity politics inherent in the American ethnic landscape, from the southern "one-drop" rule to Mexican Americans and Anglos, African American and Osage people having children, she saw to it that "the hyphen connects."

Further, Ferber's view of ethnicity as something mutable and ever-evolving resonates with Stephen Whitfield's argument that "The story of American Jews in the twentieth century can be told in terms of the erosion of a stable identity, so that eventually all of them would be described as Jews by choice" (1999, 9). In her first autobiography, the 1939 *A Peculiar Treasure*, she writes that she was inspired by the events of World War II. "The Jews of Germany, the Jews of the world, were to be destroyed. . . . I was a Jew. . . . I knew that I wanted, more than anything else, to write honestly and informatively about a family of middle-class Jews in the United States of America" (1939, 9). Ferber connected the personal to the literary in books other than her autobiographies (her second, *A Kind of Magic*, was published in 1963), with consistent pressure on questions of ethnicity throughout her work.

"By choice," in Whitfield's phrase, Ferber privileged her Jewish background, which created some problems for her. "For Doubleday, as far as promotion and sales were concerned, the book was . . . a sore spot," writes Julie Gilbert in her biography of Ferber, her great-aunt. "A story about a Jewish girl with an abundance of chutzpa and talent written at a time when Jews were being persecuted, when being a Jew, even in America was touchy was a story that Doubleday deemed as being 'special'—'not for wide appeal'" (Gilbert 1978, 291). David Biale, Michael Galchinsky, and Susan Heschel write that Jews occupy an especially fraught position because they "represent that boundary case whose very lack of belonging to a recognizable category creates a sense of unease" (5), but that "instead of bemoaning the Jews' anomalous status, we have sought to turn it into a productive virtue" (8). Ferber undertook this same challenge, and even if her Jewishness was most blatantly dealt with in her autobiographies, it also informed her novels.

Ferber's presumed lack of Jewish characters provides critics with a popular refrain: Where exactly are the Jews in this Jewish writer's work? "Although she discussed Judaism at length in her nonfiction writing, its absence from her novels has left her outside discussions of Jewish-American literature," writes Mollie Wilson. Ann Shapiro adds, "In the regional novels, Jews, if they enter the story at all, play peripheral roles" (2002, 55). And Gilbert writes that "the themes of her novels never incorporated Judaism—save for *Fanny Herself*" (1978, 112). While her novels' lead romantic characters—except, of course, Fanny—are non-Jewish, there are in fact plenty of well-realized Jewish characters in the novels, including *The Girls, Cimarron, Fanny Herself, Great Son,* and *Ice Palace.* Overlooking these specific Jewish characters elides a key aspect of Ferber's work. Ferber writes that "America—the United States, rather— seems to me to be the Jew among the nations. It is resourceful, adaptable, maligned, envied, feared, imposed upon" (1939, 13), making the country itself a Jewish-influenced space. These formerly ignored figures, I argue, require the framework of ethnicity to unpack them.

This framework informs the entwined topics of racial mixing, passing, and class that characterize so much of Ferber's work. Ferber's characters persistently quest to alter the status quo. They not only seek societal elevation, but to change society during their ascent. Her description of America as Jewish is a starting point to understanding just how mutable and vast her America is, and her prescient discussions of mixture point more, in some ways, toward today's America than toward the country she knew. Ferber's America is a complicated and unscripted space, and its resistance to definition is its most "American" quality.

Ferber's work has often been called accessible; it is also innovative not only for her portrayals of characters of various ethnicities and classes who surmount obstacles to succeed, but for her multifaceted image of American society, including its ethnic unease and insecurity. She depicted her America with huge strokes, sketching a lively and ever-changing scene. At the same time, she painted a more complicated picture. In Edna Ferber's America, ethnic and social mobility challenge any reigning order, fundamentally destabilizing the country's most rigid social systems, and imagining a place in which mixture breeds vitality and hope for the future. Her name may not have regained its early to mid-century fame, but what Ferber said about America—the way she told the story—remains relevant. Ferber's America, a place simultaneously mired in and traveling forward from its own special history, is very much the place where we still live today.

THE GIRLS
Dawn O'Hara and *Fanny Herself*

DAUNTLESS TRAVELING SALESWOMAN Emma McChesney made Edna Ferber famous. She appeared in books such as the 1913 *Roast Beef, Medium,* the 1914 *Personality Plus,* and the 1915 *Emma McChesney and Co.* as well as onstage in the 1915 play *Our Ms. McChesney.* She traveled the country, doling out lingerie samples and advice in equal portions. Emma was widely beloved. Theodore Roosevelt appreciated her as "[a]n immensely vital woman," but he did wish Emma would get married, Ferber wrote in her 1939 autobiography, *A Peculiar Treasure* (77). In the stage versions of Ferber's stories, Ethel Barrymore portrayed Emma, to whom Ferber's mother Julia referred as "Julia McFerber."

Emma's resemblance to Julia—independent, well-spoken, full of saleslady gumption—was not accidental. She was a deracinated and more upbeat version of Ferber's mother, writes Julie Gilbert (1978, 424). Just as Emma's name avoids the Jewishness that the surname "Ferber" exposes, ethnicity lurks in rather than shapes the Emma McChesney books; in the 1913 *Roast Beef, Medium,* Emma is offered a business opportunity by a "sallow, dark man" named Abe Fromkin, and she also works with a group of variously classified factory girls. The more persistent theme of these works, however, is Emma's determination and tireless pluck, the qualities that sold books and made Ferber's a household name.

People wanted to know about the woman behind Emma McChesney, and Ferber told them. Ferber believed strongly in the value of a businesswoman in society, as she told a reporter—Joyce Kilmer, of "Trees" fame—in 1915. "The butcher and the grocer and the candle-stickmaker can do what they like with the clinging vine sort of wife and mother. But they can't put much over on the wife and mother who spends six to seven hours a day in an up-to-date business office'" (1915, SM4). That same article pointed out what Ferber and Emma were up against, since Kilmer wrote that Ferber was a "daintily clad, whimsical young woman" who "looks ridiculously young" (SM4). Kilmer reminded Ferber that she had been called the inheritor of O. Henry's mantle. Her response: "When O. Henry heard that, he must have laughed" (SM5). F. Scott Fitzgerald, Matthew Bruccoli writes, added a pointed reference to ethnic background when he referred to Ferber and Fannie Hurst as "the Yiddish descendants of O. Henry" (2009, 95).

Sometimes Ferber was regarded as more than a "woman author," but, as Fitzgerald's comment indicates, she was always a Jew. And as a novelist, Ferber herself invited ethnicity into her work more than in the McChesney stories. With her longer works, she confronts bolder themes. In both the 1911 *Dawn O'Hara* and the 1917 *Fanny Herself,* the novels bracketing McChesney's heyday, Ferber applies the idea of strong womanhood so evident in her McChesney stories, and adds generous doses of autobiography. *Dawn O'Hara* is the story of a newspaperwoman, as Ferber was, and Fanny Brandeis is, like Ferber, the daughter of midwestern storekeepers. With Dawn, Emma, and Fanny, Ferber blazed a path for heroines who refused constraint by either novelistic or societal conventions. Like Emma McChesney, Dawn and Fanny must work for a living. These novels complicate that societally transgressive fact further, taking Ferber's autobiographical aspects and situating them in a larger, more systematically problematized context. Both Dawn and Fanny experience an America framed by ethnic categorization. They consistently find new ways in which their ethnicity makes them American inasmuch as it frames their own understanding of difference.

In *A Peculiar Treasure,* Ferber writes that she almost burned *Dawn O'Hara,* but her mother insisted she save it. The book was the product of a nervous breakdown Ferber suffered, and although she may have wanted to destroy it at one point, it sold well, and she evidently appreciated her mother's rescue of the manuscript. She also managed to connect the writing and breakdown in a way that shows her synthesis of life and writing when she told the writer of a "Who's Who Among Women of Big Achievement," column in the *Washington Herald* that she was actually glad she'd had the episode. It gave her the time, she told reporter Mary Mullett in 1914, to write *Dawn O'Hara*, a self-referential book about a woman reporter who has a nervous breakdown (1914, 8).

The novel is a heavily plotted story that includes romance, danger, and even some horror-show moments—Ferber later assessed it in *A Peculiar Treasure* as "sentimental and schoolgirly" (1939, 143)—but holds real complexity. The optimistically named Dawn is an Irish American woman whose appearance invites comments such as "if your [name] isn't Shaughnessy or Burke at least, then I'm no judge of what black hair and gray eyes stand for," which earns the retort of "'it happens to be O'Hara— Dawn O'Hara, if ye plaze'" (1911, 6). The American-born Dawn apes an Irish accent to emphasize her ethnicity, signaled both by her physical appearance and her accent. Dawn is thankful for her "Irish deftness" (145); she addresses herself in a brogue, "'Begorra! 'Tis losin' your sense av humor you're after doing'!" (187) and refers to her niece and nephew as the Spalpeens, a word that came to mean "rascal," but originally referred to migrant Irish workers.

While parading her Irish identity as jaunty and jovial, Dawn keeps a dark, Brontësque secret—a mentally unstable husband named Peter Orme, whom she has had placed in an asylum. "Well, one does not seek a divorce from a husband who is insane," Dawn tartly informs the reader (1911, 11). One does, however, take his job: Dawn returns to writing to support Peter. But working sickens Dawn, and she experiences a true nervous breakdown, something that had happened to Ferber in 1909: "The sight of a fly on the wall was enough to make me burst into a passion of sobs" (17). Like the novel itself, Dawn hides her introspection under a veneer of jollity. Dawn recuperates at her sister Norah's house, and Norah finds a German psychiatrist named Ernst Von Gerhart to work with Dawn. His advent initiates a discussion of Germanness, the other identity that comes to pervade the novel.

Von Gerhard feels that Dawn should give up writing for the sake of her health, and she replies that she considers herself a writer: "All of which is most unwomanly; for is not marriage woman's highest aim, and home her true sphere? . . . I was meant to be an old maid, like the terrible Kitty O'Hara. Not one of the tatting and tea kind, but an impressive, bustling old girl, with a double chin. The sharp-tongued Kitty O'Hara used to say that being an old maid was a great deal like death by drowning—a really delightful sensation when you ceased struggling" (49) Dawn's complicated approach to the idea of women's work turns preconceived notions about what is desirable for women—a home, children, a husband—upside down, since she finds becoming an "impressive, bustling old girl" more appealing. Beyond a simple message of equal rights, however, Dawn puts forth the notion that her difference—both from being a writer and living outside the domestic realm—stems from an ethnic root. Her disinclination toward inhabiting the "true sphere" is in her Irish blood, tracing back to Kitty, notably an ancestor on her paternal, unladylike side.

Further, Dawn's anticipation of the argument of true spheres, to the point that she even differentiates between "tatting and tea" and "bustling old girl" sorts of unmarried women, evinces a complex matrix of womanhood. "Norah has pleaded with me to be more like other women of my age, and for her sake I've tried" (49). She feels different, and "impressive," like the old Irish maid she emulates. "'Any woman can have a husband and babies. . . . But mighty few women can write a book. It's a special curse'" (225), she says. The refrain of the word "curse" to define her societally atypical choices demonstrates Dawn's awareness of the countercultural decisions she makes, and seems to imply that there is some sort of otherworldly rationale behind it—a "curse" rather than a choice.

Although part of his curative regimen for Dawn includes outdoor exercise, something Ferber herself loved and found restorative—and the two of them literally run hand-in-hand down the country lanes near Norah's house—Von Gerhard becomes Dawn's vector back into the diverse, urban streetscape she craves in order to fulfill these culturally atypical longings. She returns to his hometown of Milwaukee to write, and finds the German population of the city, as well as a new newspaper job, provides her desired stimulation. In Milwaukee, Germanness enriches Dawn's experience, demonstrating the multiplicity of American cities and the healthfulness of ethnic heterogeneity, which proves to serve Dawn as well as her country hikes. Dawn lives in a boarding house with German people, and remarks: "Types! I never dreamed that such faces existed outside of the old German woodcuts that one sees illustrating time-yellowed books" (79). Identity categorization provides Dawn with a way to navigate her new and plural community.

Not all of her characterizations are complimentary: Dawn anthropologically terms the German people as "aborigines" who have "bulging, knobby foreheads and bristling pompadours" (81). One wears a "bristling pompadour and [has] very small pig-eyes" (83). The German neighbors' untamed hair, marked by the wild beard and the highly styled pompadours that nevertheless "bristle," along with the animalistic "pig-eyes" coupled with the word "aborigine" suggest that Dawn sees the German boarders as somehow pre-civilized, pre-dating even her own Irish family's association with America. Her classification of their "bulging, knobby" foreheads seems an attempt to capture the ethnic high ground. None of this, however, dissuades Dawn from appreciating Milwaukee: "I felt that I was going to like it, aborigines and all" (84). Dawn's statement demonstrates the import and vitality stemming necessarily from living with a mixed group of people.

Indeed, German Milwaukee, with its variegated community, becomes a sort of extension of Von Gerhard's ability to restore Dawn's health. She admires what she sees as Germans' hale bluffness, and is astonished to see a sign on a bakery proclaiming that English is spoken within, reversing the notion that English is the default language of America's streets. In this context, Dawn serves as a prototype for later Ferber characters such as Leslie Lynnton, who marvels wide-eyed at the Mexican influence in Texas in the 1952 novel *Giant*. While Ferber well understands and describes the blends that make up America's various regions, pockets of ethnic or regional identity often shock her characters, highlighting the multiplicity of the American landscape. For her part, Dawn eventually realizes that the German-influenced Milwaukee in the novel is as much a part of America as the bucolic country lanes she wanders at her sister's house, and that she finds both invigorating. Despite Dawn's enthusiasm, her jaded editor at the newspaper finds Milwaukee's German-immersion factor uninteresting. "'But man alive, this is America!'" (1911, 91), Dawn protests, sounding much like Ferber in the more sweeping passages of her autobiographies. The editor replies, "'This isn't America. This is Milwaukee'" (91). Dawn's insistence upon Milwaukee, with its German culture, as America demonstrates her embrace of the German influence, and its fulfillment of her yen for difference.

Another non-German, the paper's sports editor Blackie Griffith, helps guide Dawn through the German neighborhoods of Milwaukee on her odyssey. Blackie's character is based upon a real sports editor named Wallie Rowland, whom Ferber knew as a reporter in Milwaukee. Blackie's use of slang, his color-based name, and his Welsh identity all contrast with the Germanic city around him, sealing his difference and allying him with the non-German Dawn. Dawn sees Blackie as slightly inhuman: "a fantastic, elfin little figure . . . [a] little brown Welshman with his lank, black hair and his deep-set, uncanny black eyes" (92), or "an amiable brown gnome, or a cheerful little joss-house god come to life" (98), with the idea of the joss-house, or Chinese folk temple, cementing Blackie's identity as different. For his part, Blackie refers to his own "'Spanish style of beauty'" (121), but the "hot, painful red dyeing Blackie's sallow face" betrays his unrequited love for Dawn (276).

Blackie exposes Dawn to German life at a bakery where "[t]here was nothing about the place or its occupants to remind one of America. This dim, smoky, cake-scented café was Germany" (111). How to assimilate this seeming contradiction preoccupies Dawn's Milwaukee experience, with the bakery, in which Dawn must gesture and draw pictures to order the pastries she wants, as a symbol. Mostly, Dawn marvels at how no other patrons find their surroundings queer, and Blackie responds, "'Sure not; that's the beauty of it. They don't need to make no artificial atmosphere for this place; it just grows wild, like dandelions'" (116). Blackie's observation demonstrates his plural worldview. In his mind, there is nothing anomalous about a German-only bakery in the midst of the American heartland. Its organic appearance from the German community makes it natural, as his weed metaphor emphasizes. Indeed, Blackie chooses Germany as a vacation spot, "knowin' that it would feel homelike there" (102). Blackie's Welshness keeps him alongside Dawn as an outsider in Milwaukee, a position he seems more at ease maintaining than she does. Ultimately, Dawn and Blackie decide "we're not caring so long as we approve of one another" (252), underscoring the need each has for some sort of communal society.

Dawn also befriends her German fellow-boarders, particularly the women. The "lady aborigines," as she thinks of them, admire Dawn's clothing and request her help selecting their own wardrobes. This plotline becomes a commentary on the anything-can-happen nature of American society, as Dawn at first plays the role of a lady bountiful, doling out clothes and fashion advice. One beneficiary has fled Germany because of a star-crossed marriage to a lower-class man. But he disapproves of the new clothes. "[I]n Amerika all things are different," she says (152). With her spunk, this woman becomes, in Dawn's estimation, "the plucky little aborigine who, with the donning of the new Amerikanische gown had acquired some real Amerikanische nerve" (154). Like Dawn, Frau Nirlanger flaunts convention, and this sequence inverts the American bootstrap myth—Frau Nirlanger loses social status by immigrating—and also reinforces the notion of equality in what is still enough of a shifting, categorized country that Dawn considers herself an Irishwoman in a German city. The "aborigine" is really an Austrian noblewoman, but Dawn imagines her as uncivilized. Dawn also describes her as "plucky" and "little," words easily applied to a new immigrant who adapts quickly to her new country and makes good. Milwaukee may seem German, but it's not, really. Instead, it takes America itself to give Frau Nirlanger "nerve." America becomes the great leveler, bringing the Austrian aristocrat to her husband's more plebian caste. At the same time, it gives the noblewoman the ability to transcend and simultaneously use her elevated class and acquired nerve to take on her husband.

Dawn is saved from internalizing this lesson when her husband Peter returns, and the novel concludes with a predictable tragedy that leaves Dawn free to marry Von Gerhard. In *Dawn O'Hara*, healthful mixture requires a German American man (and city) combined with an Irish American heroine. With Dawn's acclimatization of Germanness in both location and spouse, Ferber moves toward the concept of heterogeneity as strengthening rather than diluting. Both participants are notably white, while future novels included both cultural and ethnic blending, but with the happy couple poised to initiate a dynasty of nationally hybridized children, the novel nevertheless prefigures the plots of many of Ferber's regional novels. "'Coming, Kindchen?'" (302), Von Gerhard asks Dawn at the end of the book, his German endearment setting the stage for her future as a part of the German community.

If Ferber acknowledged such *Dawn O'Hara* moments as the character of Blackie and the locale of Brumbach's as direct allusions her own experience, *Fanny Herself* pushes much farther into autobiography. At one point in her actual autobiography *A Peculiar Treasure*, rather than

describe an episode, Ferber simply reprints a passage from *Fanny Herself.*
As she writes, "A good deal of it was imaginary, a good deal of it was real"
(1939, 202). There is, however, more to the novel than a simple reprisal
of Ferber's coming of age. For one, *Fanny Herself* includes some particularly self-conscious moments of departure from the Emma McChesney
books, most notably when Emma herself appears as a cameo, stopping
through Fanny's family's store on a sales call (1917, 90). In an almost
postmodern touch, Ferber writes of a character's brogue, "There shall be
no vain attempt to set it down. Besides, you always skip dialect" (118).
Ferber pokes fun at her own earlier writing; she understands what hackneyed phrases (a staple of the six-years-previous *Dawn O'Hara*) a more
sophisticated reader—the reader of *Fanny Herself*—will "always skip."

More importantly, *Fanny Herself* deals frankly with Fanny's ethnicity
and offers explicit and complicated images of American Jewishness. In
an article in *MELUS*, Carol Batker calls *Fanny Herself* Ferber's "most Jewish novel" (2000, 91). The text offers a complex reading of Jewishness,
including descriptions of passing and anti-Semitism, and explodes some
stereotypes along the way. When it was published, readers understood
its Jewish characterizations to uphold derogatory labels. "Mother and
daughter are fine women; the son's lack of consideration of them may be
the Jewish attitude toward women," wrote the anonymous reviewer in a
New York Sun article called "Critical Reviews of the Season's Latest Fiction." (1917, 6). Nevertheless, the review sees *Fanny Herself* as the "best
and most substantial work she [Ferber] has turned out" (6).

Fanny Herself stands as an argument for Jewish diversity, upending
societally dictated generalizations and pointing the way toward a future
where there are as many different American Jews as there are Americans.
The novel tells the story of Fanny Brandeis, the daughter of storekeepers in a midwestern town dubbed Winnebago. As in Ferber's own life,
Fanny's father is infirm, and her mother runs the family dry-goods store.
Their town is small, with Fanny and one friend "the only two in her room
at school who stayed out on the Day of Atonement" (1917, 24), but large
enough to support a local synagogue. Jewishness is a fundamental part of
Fanny's identity as a "sensitive, highly-organized, dramatic little Jewish
girl," an "emotional little Jewess" (29), and "a little Jew girl, with whole
centuries of suffering behind one" (42).

Ferber calls Fanny a "little Oriental" (25) a reference to Jewishness to which she returns in the 1930 novel *Cimarron*, and which provides an opening into a much larger context. In their introduction to *Orientalism and the Jews*, Ivan Davidson Kalmar and Derek J. Penslar write, "The romantic image of a noble oriental Jew" cropped up from the late eighteenth to early twentieth centuries, and Ferber's use of the term 'oriental' for her Jewish characters resonates within this tradition" (2005, xviii). According to Kalmar and Penslar, "On the Jewish side, [orientalism] was seized upon by a desire to proclaim the Jews as a 'race' or 'nation' of great antiquity, ennobled by its association with the Bible, but also more generally with the Orient as the source of spiritual inspiration for the West" (xxviii). Although Ferber was, of course, American, her use of the word reveals an inheritance of a European "bourgeois" tradition. This image of the oriental, noble Jew, which Ferber paraphrases in her autobiographies, motivates not only her characters but also the ethnically concerned novels themselves. In later works, the concept of the "oriental," or ancient and respected culture, pervades ethnic groups beyond Jews, as one of Ferber's consistently allusive points of rhetoric relies upon claiming a culture as venerable or "oriental." "The Jews . . . felt that their race, the Chosen People who brought knowledge of God to the world, was perhaps the noblest of them all," write Kalman and Penslar (xxix), historicizing this view within the eighteenth century. Ferber carries it into the twentieth, beginning with the direct association of *Fanny Herself*—and Ferber herself—with this tradition.

One of the seminal childhood moments in Fanny's association with orientalism comes from fasting on Yom Kippur, the holiest day on the Jewish calendar. Ferber paints the incident, in which Fanny refuses even the most tempting delicacies, as shaping her personality, demonstrating that her strength of character emanates from her Jewishness. Young children are not even expected to fast on Yom Kippur, so the self-denial serves even further to elevate the achievement of Fanny, the "little oriental." In another ennobled and ennobling moment, the young Fanny defends a fellow Jewish child named Clarence Heyl whom young bullies are calling "the Name," code for an ethnic slur (1917, 44) which is most likely "sheeny," the word Ferber recalls hearing in *A Peculiar Treasure* (1939, 40).

As Fanny grows, the novel participates in some rhetoric akin to "the Name": the age-old self-loathing belief that somehow it is better not to "look Jewish." (Ferber herself reportedly underwent rhinoplasty.) Fanny is "not what is known as the Jewish type, in spite of her coloring" (1917, 91). Yet Fanny compares herself only to characters with self-consciously Jewish surnames. "What do you want me to do? Stay here, and grub away, and become a crabbed old maid like Irma Klein . . . or I could marry a traveling man, perhaps, or Lee Kohn of the Golden Eagle" (120). Her experience allows her to ruminate, but possibility for the future is relentlessly couched in Jewish terms. (Notably, for example, Fanny never says she could emulate Emma McChesney—who drops by the Brandeis store—to fuse the Irma Klein and Lee Kohn identities into a familiar traveling female salesperson.) Jewishness preoccupies Fanny's character.

Fanny's mother dies, a plot decision with which Ferber was displeased: "The first half [of *Fanny Herself*] is good," Ferber writes in *A Peculiar Treasure.* "The second half is weak and floundering. The trouble was that in the middle of the book I killed Molly Brandeis because she was walking off with the story under the heroine's very eyes" (1939, 202). Ferber may have missed Molly's presence—or perhaps she was simply feeling guilty about killing off a character who shared so much with her own mother—but the novel actually gains scope after Molly's death, as what Ferber deems "floundering" leads to some pointed interrogations of Jewishness. "'Your mother, Fanny, we didn't understand her so well, here in Winnebago, among us Jewish ladies,'" says the rabbi's wife. "'She was different'" (1917, 125). Ferber's Winnebago is a provincial enough place to allow taunting of a Jewish boy, but also large enough for "different"—if not always comfortable—Jewish identities, from the homemakers to storekeeper Molly Brandeis. With her pugnacity, Fanny also is "different," befriending the local priest. However, this association is also couched within Jewishness, and Father Fitzpatrick's assistant turns her away, because she is "not a parishioner." Father Fitzpatrick rebukes the assistant, but the episode cements Fanny's position as an outsider. Father Fitzpatrick's explanation:

> "You're different. And I'll tell you why. You're a Jew."
> "Yes, I've got that handicap."

"That isn't a handicap, Fanny. It's an asset. Outwardly you're like any other girl of your age. Inwardly you've been molded by occupation, training, religion, history, temperament, race, into something—." (120)

Neither Jews nor Catholics were especially popular with the majority white Protestant culture in America at the time of the characters' conversation, yet Fanny casts her own position as "handicapped," even to a priest who might feel similarly burdened.

Father Fitzpatrick's description of Jews focuses on how their difficult past as a people impacts their daily lives: "'You've suffered, you Jews, for centuries and centuries, until you're all artists—quick to see drama because you've lived in it, emotional, oversensitive, cringing, or swaggering, high-strung, demonstrative, affectionate, generous" (122). For the priest, Jewishness becomes a multifaceted identity with negative—"cringing"—and positive—"generous"—features, all within a temperamental artist's framework. His understanding of an ethnicity continues to fit the definition of "oriental," with its background of centuries of pain.

Ignoring Father Fitzpatrick's prescient advice that she pursue an artistic career, Fanny instead seeks a decidedly prosaic job at a clothing company. Her boss, Mr. Fenger, puts her on the spot when she acts "poetic," behavior that evidently constitutes an ethnic signal.

"Jew?" he asked.

A breathless instant. "No," said Fanny Brandeis. Michael Fenger smiled for the first time. Fanny Brandeis would have given everything she had, everything she hoped to be, to be able to take back that monosyllable. She was gripped with horror at what she had done. She had spoken almost mechanically. And yet that monosyllable must have been the fruit of all these months of inward struggle and thought. "Now I begin to understand you," Fenger went on. "You've decided to lop off all the excrescences, eh? Well, I can't say that I blame you. A woman in business is handicapped enough by the fact of her sex" (136).

Fenger catches Fanny in the act of "lopping off" parts of her identity to avoid participating as both woman and Jew—and praises her for it. Fanny regrets her attempt to pass almost the moment it happens, yet understands that at some level she does strive to abandon Jewishness. This uneasy embrace comes at a cost. Lying about her identity presents Fanny as morally suspect, which is in turn read as sexually available to the married Fenger. She rejects him and chastises herself. "'You lied to him on that very first day. . . . Now he thinks you're rotten all the way through'" (153). The "rottenness" Fanny imagines includes both her Jewishness and the ethical instability Fenger assumes. The interaction underlines the crucial nature of Fanny's Jewishness to her identity.

Fanny's ideas about her ethnicity are further complicated by the return of Clarence Heyl, the fellow Jew whom Fanny rescued from bullies as a child in Wisconsin. Clarence has transformed from a sickly child to an intrepid outdoorsman and nature writer (128). Like the prescient Father Fitzpatrick, Clarence believes Fanny should give up her life in business to become an artist, and says:

> "I tell you, Fanny, we Jews have got a money-grubbing, loud-talking, diamond-studded, get-there-at-any-price reputation, and perhaps we deserve it. But every now and then, out of the mass of us, one lifts his head and stands erect, and the great white light is in his face. And that person has suffered, for suffering breeds genius. . . . You see it all the way from Lew Fields to Sarah Bernhardt; from Mendelssohn to Irving Berlin; to Mischa Elman to Charlie Chaplin. . . . You're cutting yourself off from your own people—a dramatic, impulsive, emotional people" (189–90).

The claim Heyl lays at Fanny's feet resembles the one critics would later level at Ferber: that her fiction was somehow lacking in Jewishness. His point—echoing Father Fitzpatrick's—that "suffering breeds genius" resonates with Ferber's comment in her autobiography *A Peculiar Treasure*: "again and again deprived of property or liberty . . . we [Jews] have turned to the one thing . . . creative self-expression" (1939, 57). With his layering of adjectives such as "emotional" and "dramatic," over his understanding of the majority culture's claim that Jewish people are "money-grubbing" and "diamond-studded," Clarence evinces his own nuanced insider's understanding of American Jewishness, and encourages Fanny to place herself outside the category of stereotype, even as it frames their own struggles for identity.

Further, Heyl's list presents a roster of those who also surpassed merely ethnic identification to become American artists. The passage demonstrates the contributions Jewish people, from violinist Elman to actress Bernhardt, made to contemporary American society. This passage demonstrates his internalization of the era's ideas about Jews, with all the attendant stereotypes that Clarence enumerates along with the honor roll of Jewish American artists. Additionally complicating *Fanny Herself* is that Clarence—and Ferber—never disavow the acknowledged stereotype entirely. As Jewish artists themselves, these sympathetic characters— which include Fanny, Clarence, and Sarah Berhardt—are portrayed as differing from the masses and are graced with a notably "white" light, in a syntactic move that reinstates rather than dismisses the harsher stereotypes. Instead of conveying positive images of Charlie Chaplin as Jewish, for example, there remains the mass of unappealingly "diamond-studded" Jewish people. The chosen, artistic few may rise above them, but the harsh characterizations remain. Fanny, for example, denies her heritage to Mr. Fenger so she would not be perceived as money-grubbing, not to avoid being mistaken for Sarah Bernhardt.

This anxiety is furthered by Fanny's nickname for Clarence. Despite his resembling, as Fanny says, "'one of the minor Hebrew prophets, minus the beard,'" she insists upon calling Clarence by the Irish-identified surname, "Clancy" (187), because "'I can't call you Clarence. It doesn't fit.'" The name-changing, although depicted as a playful, flirtatious exchange, also hearkens to the many "lopped-off" Jewish names (although "Clarence" does not fall into this category) as well as Fanny's abortive earlier attempt to pass as non-Jewish. Names are particularly relevant in a Jewish context, since they are so often used as signifiers. If Clarence's name "doesn't fit," then what about his Jewishness?

Coupled with vexed moments such as these is the depiction of Fanny's housekeeper, Princess, who "was royal in name only—a biscuit-tinted lady, with a very black and no-account husband," which adds another layer of racial disquiet to Fanny's own ethnic navigations (177). As Batker writes of *Fanny Herself*, "racist rhetoric . . . pervades the text. . . . [T]he Japanese servant of Fenger's is termed "sneaking," and Fanny's African

American domestic servant's "black" husband is read as lazy ("Literary Reformers," 2000, 93). Princess also speaks in dialect, calling Clarence a "gep'mun" (1917, 177). Even as Ferber defines pathways out of the Jewish "mass" for Fanny and Clarence, Princess remains little more than a two-dimensional cutout of an African American servant.

Clarence's character, masculine and less burdened than Fanny, stands as Ferber's example of ways to break down the "money-grubbing" stereotype. He seizes upon an American archetype and pioneers westward to Colorado. When he becomes a nature writer, eschewing the indoor occupations (rabbi, storekeeper, salesman) of the Jewish people in Winnebago, he places himself into a literary category that could render him one of those listed in his own "white light" speech. Clarence is something of a "little Oriental" himself. Batker writes that Clarence "exemplifies . . . distance from urban Jewish immigrants and [Ferber's] desire to combine Jewish and American identities" ("Literary Reformers," 2000, 93). The desire to rise above the masses becomes truth. With their artistic careers elevating them above the hordes, Fanny and Clarence no longer need to fit into pigeonholes, but can join the elevated, white-light-illuminated group of Jews.

With Clarence's influence, Fanny undoes her attempt to pass, redeeming herself from the shame of that moment. She draws a portrait of an old Jewish man that provokes Clarence's comment: "'It took a thousand years of suffering and persecution and faith to stamp that look on his face'" (1917, 159). When, later, Fenger later asks Fanny how she learned so much about people "in such a short time," she replies, "'It hasn't been a short time. . . . It took a thousand years'" (222). Fenger is "puzzled" by this response (222). But for Fanny, the echo of the "thousand years" represents a clear allusion not only to Clarence's remark, but also to her earlier effort to conceal her Jewishness from her boss. The notion of the long-suffering Jewish man coupled with Fanny's comment restores the idea of the "oriental" Fanny, patiently fasting while lesser children eat. Since the conversation is with Fenger, for whom she attempted the pass, her deliverance is complete.

The "thousand years" line of argument, of course, long predates Ferber's use. Victorian-era British Prime Minister Benjamin Disraeli once rebutted a slur with: "Yes, I am a Jew, and when the ancestors of mine right honorable gentleman were brutal savages in an unknown island, mine were priests in the temple of Solomon" (qtd. in Bartlett 1992, 434). Judah P. Benjamin, who was the treasurer of the Confederacy, told an antagonist: "The gentleman will please remember that when his half-civilized ancestors were hunting the wild boar in the forests of Silesia, mine were the princes of the earth" (qtd. in Bartlett 1992, 434n). And Justice Louis D. Brandeis wrote in his pamphlet, *A Call To The Educated Jew*, that "The Torah led the "People of the Book" to intellectual pursuits at times when most of the Aryan peoples were illiterate" (1915, 59). Ferber's invocation of this rhetoric, coupled with Orientalism, demonstrates her view of Jewishness as aligned with Jews as culturally ancient and worthy of veneration.[1]

Becoming more self-consciously Jewish fulfills Fanny's need for artistic expression. Clarence, like Father Fitzpatrick, encourages her to abandon her work in the fashion industry, opting instead to defend and uplift Jewish immigrants through her journalistic illustration. The tension between stereotype and representation comes to the forefront with this new career: "She prowled in the Ghetto, and sketched those patient Jewish faces, often grotesque, sometimes repulsive, always mobile," Ferber writes (1917, 160). Jewish faces show "the courage of a race serene in the knowledge that it cannot die" (250). The lack of facile resolution of Fanny's conflict acts as a microcosm of the very anxiety—grotesque or serene? repulsive or courageous?—that motivates the novel's interrogation of Jewishness.

This struggle aptly reflects Ferber's initial forays, in *Dawn O'Hara* and *Fanny Herself*, into the exploration of American identity politics. Dawn and Fanny must struggle with the ethnic categorizations that focus their own characters and the books themselves. For Dawn, the idea of challenging societal expectations to become a writer and of inviting an American brand of Germanness to invigorate her Irish-identified life demon-

1. Ferber argued in conversation as well as in her books that Jewishness deserves respect. Dorothy Rodgers (the wife of composer Richard Rodgers) told a story about having Ferber at a dinner party while some other guests made comments about Jews being unable to achieve certain heights: "Edna said, 'Well, one of our boys made it'—meaning Jesus, and it was a marvelously well-taken point that Jesus was a Jew. And she was witty and forceful and very clear about it" (Gilbert 1978, 64).

strates a milder version of the integrative narratives that would come in regional novels such as *Show Boat* and *Saratoga Trunk*. Likewise, Fanny's grappling with both representation and internalization of Jewishness shows the pervasiveness of stereotype as well as the consistent and latent possibility of its implosion.

Ferber's readiness both to frame and invalidate societal codes in *Dawn O'Hara* and *Fanny Herself* establishes the key tension within her multifaceted work. Characters exist both within and without their determined roles, using ethnicity as a lever to lift and negotiate larger questions of American society and its internally fraught quest both to frame and explode the various categories to which an individual can—and chooses to—belong.

2

WHEAT AND EMERALDS
The Girls and *So Big*

THE CITY OF CHICAGO, where Ferber lived from 1909 to 1922, houses some of her diversifying ethnic portrayals as the original homes of the protagonists of the 1921 *The Girls* and of *So Big*, published in 1924. This city, an appropriately sprawling and heterogeneous place for Ferber's enmeshed, overlapping plotlines, becomes both a framing device and a representative site of ethnic intersections in these two early novels. Like *Fanny Herself*, both books are often read as offering piquant examples of Ferber's strong women, since each book focuses on powerful female characters. These accomplished women direct businesses, harvest crops, go off to war, and otherwise demonstrate contemporary gender role–transgressing abilities and independence. Besides these crucial representations of womanhood, however, each novel is also preoccupied with ethnic and class taxonomy, and the ways in which these striations shape both individuals and societies.

With these two novels, Ferber demonstrated the intrinsic necessity of heterogeneous influence to the health of American culture. Her representations of different ethnicities and groupings stem naturally from her focus particularly on Jewish and German people in *Fanny Herself* and *Dawn O'Hara*. In *The Girls* and *So Big*, however, Ferber begins to explore the questions of what happens to ethnic identities in America when they outgrow dedicated neighborhoods such as the German one in *Dawn O'Hara*'s Milwaukee. *The Girls* includes representations of proliferating identities while *So Big* adds tension between rural and urban Americas, and the overarching spectrum of class proves the increasingly complex matrix of identity politics involved in being—and becoming—American.

The Girls concerns a matriarchal Chicago family who showcases Ferber's characters' determination to overcome societal mandates. The novel is a clear inheritor of Ferber's previous work and the concerns that became more patent throughout the Emma McChesney stories, *Dawn O'Hara* and *Fanny Herself*, with resolute women who ignore social protocol—and proclaim their defiance—at its center. "Its background was to be Chicago, its chief characters three old maids of three generations in one family, all alive and each representing the American woman of her day," Ferber decided before she began writing (*A Peculiar Treasure* [1939], 233). The "old maids" of *The Girls* resemble the women to whose reputation Dawn O'Hara claims to aspire—"impressive, bustling old girl[s]" (1911, 49). Ferber was proud of her work. "*The Girls* was a mature novel," she writes in *A Peculiar Treasure*. "I felt it marked a definite advance and that it was by a large margin the best piece of writing I had done up to now" (1939, 237).

To write the novel, Ferber rented an apartment facing Lake Michigan. The lake, the story goes, was so beautiful that she couldn't concentrate. Her publisher advised her to turn her desk around so it faced the wall, and she was able to get on with the book, she wrote Rogers Dickinson, who quoted her in a pamphlet, *Edna Ferber, A Sketch* (1925, 8). He also quoted her strong feelings about Chicago: "Chicago, sprawled over miles of prairie like a great, uncouth, sooty-faced, huge-limbed (see Sandburg poems) giant, cannot be traversed easily" (21). In these early years, she still considered Chicago home. Even though she lived in New York, she would never be more than an "onlooker. . . . [W]hen it comes to writing I turn back to the town with a little human awkwardness left in it" (26). Ferber eschewed easy answers in favor of more problematic settings and societal issues that present no facile solutions.

The protagonists of *The Girls* find themselves going against trends in the midst of vexed times. Despite their more defying attitudes, they stand as original members of Chicago's late-blooming and precipitous high society, as "Chicago South Siders since that September in 1836 when Isaac Thrift had traveled" (1921, 5). The Girls themselves are some of the most ethnically bland of Ferber's characters. For the generations of Thrift women—the family patronymic hearkens to a quintessentially American value, overlaid with the idea of the Puritan work ethic—class functions as a uniquely American condition, something changeable at a near-daily rate. Many of the women are named Charlotte, and given various nicknames to distinguish one from the next, a pattern that Ferber uses in many of her dynastic novels, including *American Beauty, Cimarron,* and *Come and Get It.* This makes for confusing reading, but the double and triple naming of characters serves to emphasize continuity within families and the formation of an American people. Also, the same names, once distilled into a variety of pet names, serve to underscore differences between similarly named individuals and their widely variant generational attitudes.

In *The Girls,* much of this mutability relies upon a lower-class Dutch American family named Dick, whose men attract Thrift and Payson women of different generations. Poets, workers, and soldiers, the Dicks threaten the patrician Thrift name of subsequent Charlottes, but ultimately their influence infuses the Girls with resolve, even if their relationships tend to halt abruptly. In *The Girls,* class sometimes stands in for the vibrant ethnic identity—Irish, German or Jewish, for Dawn O'Hara and Fanny Brandeis—needed to invigorate an anemic "American" family. Ferber presents Chicago as a fluctuating society, where ethnic and class interlopers derail any attempt to establish an upper class, and can themselves become that class. This transience also allows for a uniquely American town: "The names of Chicago's firemen of 1838 or '40, if read aloud today, would sound like the annual list of box-holders at the opera," Ferber writes (1921, 16). With this characterization, she demonstrates the ease of elision in American society, where blue-collar workers can rapidly ascend to the upper class.

Such instability leads to various segments of society colliding, as when the lower-class Jesse Dick rescues Charlotte from the icy river as a child, and then rescues her yet again when she falls into a swampy area. Despite their melodramatic meetings, his family presents trouble: The Dicks are a group of "nobodies. In a day when social lines were so elastic as to be nearly all-inclusive the Dicks were miles beyond the pale" (23). Ferber's description of the lines as "elastic" brings the novel's anxiety into focus: the lines may be changeable, but they remain strong. The motivating tension of *The Girls* is built upon the difference between firefighters and operagoers, those who achieve higher status and those who, like the Dicks, remain mired in lower-class life despite the considerable energy some members display.

This class assignation chafes at people like Jesse Dick, who, although he had "sprung from this soil, still was alien to it; a dreamer; a fawn among wallowing swine" (23). Even within the novel's "elastic" Chicago, some people are still deemed "swine." Just as restricting (if not as harshly termed) are the lessons Charlotte internalizes from her upper-class upbringing: "Years of narrow nagging bound her with bands of steel riveted with turn-your-toes-out, hold-your-shoulders-back, you-mustn't-play-with-them, ladylike, ladylike" (32). The repressive rearing physically affects Charlotte's body. The nameless "them" with whom she "mustn't play" is a clear reference to the Dick family and other members of the lower classes who have not yet accomplished the climb to the opera box. This version of America allows glimpses of mobility, but also underscores the capricious—and financially dependent—nature of some social status changes. Fire-fighters may become operagoers, but they need money to accomplish the change.

Thus, Charlotte keeps her love for Jesse Dick secret. He counters her view of him as low-class with the line of rhetoric that Ferber originally assigned to Jewishness and is well used by Ferber characters: "the Dicks came from Holland. I mean a long time ago. With Hendrik Hudson'" (33). This comment serves to underline the importance of being an old family—using the same rhetoric as that protecting "oriental" Jews—while also exposing the Thrifts' hypocrisy. Typically, those who claim an ancestor as aureate as Henry Hudson (and Jesse's use of the Dutch "Hendrik" forces into play the authenticity of the national background they share) would, if anything, be more elevated in society than the 1836-arriving Isaac Thrift to whose coattails the family clings. Yet in the Chicago of *The Girls*, ancestry matters less than the current state of a family's financial health, so that being related to Hendrik (Henry) Hudson holds less sway than holding an opera box now.

Despite inborn misgivings about her star-crossed relationship, a passion-swept Charlotte kisses Jesse in the street as he heads off to war, eliciting incoherent condemnation: "ruined her life . . . brought down disgrace . . . common lout like a Dick . . . Dick! . . . Dick!" (38). Repeating the name histrionically seems to emphasize the crushing blow that Charlotte has given the Thrifts with her affection for Jesse. The name Dick, synonymous with "common lout," demonstrates the Paysons' depth of feeling at what they consider their daughter's betrayal, even with her slight, if allusive, act. "Of Charlotte's impulsive act her father and mother made something repulsive and sinister," Ferber writes (42). Jesse Dick dies in the war, so the kiss never results in a lasting arrangement, but Charlotte remains tainted by their illicit connection, bogged down by even this briefest of associations with a lower-class man.

Ferber's description of the Thrifts remains somewhat sympathetic despite her depiction of their overreaction to Charlotte and Jesse's kiss: "Had they been as wise and understanding as they were well-meaning, these two Calvinistic parents might have cured Charlotte by one visit to the Dicks' Hardscrabble kitchen, with a mangy cur nosing her skirts; a red-faced hostess at the washtub; and a ruined, battered, travesty of the slim young rhyme-making Jesse Dick there in the person of old Pete Dick squatting, sodden, in the doorway" (51). This grim description of the Dicks' life collides with the Thrifts' vision of what fate could have befallen Charlotte. The passage recalls the earlier mention of "swine," with people who live in a kitchen sullied by a dirty dog, promoting a sort of deserved credibility to their deprived lot in life. With this description of the Dicks' apartment, class seems less arbitrarily assigned and more appropriate, as if the washtub, doorway, and dog conspired to keep the family down. "Squatting" in the doorway gives the impression of someone there without permission, and if the drunken Pete Dick is no more than a "travesty" of his son, Jesse's fate seems sealed. Had Jesse not died in the war, Ferber implies, he could have become simply another common lout, "ruined" and "battered"—both adjectives describing time-consuming processes—by life. The servile Mrs. Dick is depicted as washing her own clothes to contrast with Charlotte, whose own fine clothes are presumably laundered by maids. Jesse's poetry is denigrated to mere "rhyme" to convey its meaninglessness, and even the family dog is portrayed as a mangy cur engaging in the off-color canine behavior of skirt nosing.

Charlotte's beleaguered sister Carrie attempts to escape either a fate of genteel poverty or of stultification by marrying Samuel Payson, the suitor Charlotte, still besotted with her handsome Jesse, refuses because he reminds her of Uriah Heep, the groveling, obsequious clerk in Charles Dickens's *David Copperfield,* one of Ferber's favorite books. Samuel also loses the family fortune, so, as Julia Ferber did, Carrie becomes a businesswoman. This sequence of events costs her her femininity. "Her fingers were heavy, clumsy, almost rough, like a man's," Ferber writes (1921, 65). The household, however, maintains its respectability even without funds and with the taint of commercialism that Carris must shoulder: "'One of the Thrift girls' might mean anyone in the Prairie Avenue household, but it was never anything but a term of respect and meant much to anyone who was native to Chicago" (66). "Girls" may be a "term of respect," but it is also infantilizing, suggesting that the women in the Thrift family suffer from a group attack of arrested development, never truly achieving full maturity.

In this urban microcosm, once the Jesse Dick wedge is driven in and then enlarged by the family's lack of money, the Thrifts' world widens to include ethnic variation. The intersection of class and ethnicity results in a Dickensian twist that would have horrified the original Thrifts, when Lottie (Charlotte's niece and namesake) dates a Jew named Rutherford Hayes Adler. "Ford" is Jewish in the Fanny and Clarence mold, bright as Bernhardt, a multitalented scholar and novelist. Yet, like Fanny and Clarence, he is not depicted glowingly. Instead, Ferber writes, "Being swarthy, black-haired, and black-eyed he was cursed with a taste for tan suits and red neckties. These, with the high choker collar of the period, gave him the look of an endman strayed from the minstrel troupe" (74). In Ford's appearance, Jewishness is colluded not only with African Americanness, but also with a performance in which the white members of a minstrel troupe "blacked up" to appear African American. As Eric Lott writes in his 1995 study of minstrelsy, *Love and Theft,* "At every turn blackface minstrelsy has seemed a form in which transgression and containment coexisted" (234). Lott's work focuses on antebellum minstrelsy, but Ford's inability to blend in with the society around him—standing out in his loud, inappropriate clothing, for example—combines with illicit overlays of carnival, so that his appearance, like that of a blackface minstrel, evades anything genuine. Ford's complexion, Ferber's description suggests, makes him look as if he is in costume, giving his character a cast of inauthenticity that contrasts sharply with the actions he takes when Lottie's mother, Carrie Payson (Charlotte's sister), demands his name. The "Rutherford Hayes" portion of his name demonstrates that American Jews are good immigrants who shuck off their old-world identities to name their children after American presidents, but Ford's surname announces his ethnicity to the disdainful Carrie: "The boy had heard that tone used many times in the past nineteen hundred years. 'Adler,' he replied" (76). Like Fanny, whose understanding of the past "thousand" years is bound up in Jewish tradition, Ford bears his heritage consciously.

Further uncomfortable identity probing reveals that Ford's father's middle name was Isaac. As Carrie pieces together his background, he remembers that her father's name was Isaac, too. With her reply—"An altogether different kind of Isaac, you would have thought. No relation to the gentleman in the Bible. A New England Isaac not to be confused with the Levantine of that name" (1921, 76)—Ferber exposes American hypocrisy, housed in Carrie's over-sensitive snobbishness. Carrie is blind to Ford and Ferber's point that the name Isaac was in noble use far before even the most patrician American lived.

> "I don't remember ever having seen [your grandfather] mentioned in books on early Chicago."
>
> "You wouldn't," said Adler; "he isn't."
>
> "And why not?"
>
> "Jews," said Rutherford Hayes, pleasantly, and laconically.
>
> Mrs. Payson stood up. So did the boy. He had no difficulty in rising now. No self-consciousness, no awkwardness. There was about him suddenly a fluid grace, an easy muscular rhythm. (77)

With his announcement, Ford relaxes. By performing the opposite of Fanny's passing attempt—a continued insistence on his Jewishness—Ford finds satisfaction and even physical comfort in his "fluid grace." Surmounting the kind of constant anti-Semitism Carrie displays, Ford achieves fame as a writer, furthering his association with the elevated group of Jews—musicians, poets, artists—that Clarence Heyl lists to encourage Fanny.

Furthering the already belabored but continually unfolding point of Ford's Jewish/Oriental virtue, Ferber includes a backward-looking plot device: the ancestors Abraham Isaac Adler and Isaac Thrift are acquaintances. In fact, in a deliberate reversal of the stereotype of Jews as financially acquisitive, Ford's grandfather loses his own fortune when the hapless Payson ruins a firm in which the elder Adler invests. Even in the face of all of these sterling qualities, including what many would see as familial obligation to right an ancient wrong, Carrie forbids the obedient Lottie to date Ford, even though Lottie is "[b]raver—not much, but still braver—than Charlotte had been before her" (78). Lottie concedes, not fierce enough to do as she pleases, like her aunt allowing exciting and virtuous men to pass by, preferring familial approval and validating the class structure imposed on them by Chicago.

As with Charlotte, refusing an early love affair results in a stilted existence so that Lottie settles in to a life of caring for her mother and nieces. The gender issues that frame *The Girls* continue to intersect with ethnic restrictions, as one of Lottie's single friends has a similar experience to Lottie's adolescent one, a minor incident that nevertheless reflects the larger, more overarching concerns of the novel and emphasizes the ways in which Ferber demonstrates the effects of a hegemonic society. The friend claims no need for a husband because her work fills her life, and another, named Beck, retorts: "that didn't keep you from wanting to marry that brainy little kike Socialist over on the West Side; and it didn't keep your people from interfering and influencing you, and making your life so miserable that you hadn't the spirit left to—" (109). Whether in the shape of the unhandsome-to-graceful, brilliant Ford or the "brainy little kike Socialist," Jewishness presents an "obstacle." Jewish men appear, attract gentile women, and force them to obey the strictures of their parents rather than their own sentiments. Otherwise self-sufficient women cannot defy authority to associate with Jews, despite their appeal and the changing times or social mobility publicly declaimed in local culture.

Revealing the ways in which hypocrisy mars Chicago society, these women, however, seem to learn little from their experiences with the damaging and stultifying effects of bigotry. Beck's very speech including the mention of the "kike Socialist" is interrupted by a call to lunch from "a South Side Hebe—her ebony face grotesque between the lacy cap and apron with which Celia had adorned her for the day" (113). The image recalls American slavery, which had ended only about sixty years before, with the objectified domestic worker treated as something to be "adorned," just like the rest of the apartment. The adjective "grotesque" suggests an understanding of the unnatural way in which the African American servant is treated, and the idea of her as Hebe, the cup-bearer of the gods in Greco-Roman mythology, reflects this lack of humanity. The friends may understand the bigotry of the episode with the "kike Socialist," but the tensions inherent in a racially bound society exist within the text.

Throughout the novel, in fact, servants evoke tension with their othered ethnic status, whether African American, Scandinavian, or Slavic, all parts of the profusion of ethnicities Ferber includes in these early works. This occurs in small ways—Carrie Payson blames the fact that her maid Hulda drinks too much coffee on Swedish heritage—and large, as when Lottie takes in Jennie, seventeen-year-old sister of the maid Gussie, whose "thick-tongued speech told of her Slavic origin" (178). When Lottie rescues Jennie from the Chicago legal system, the courtroom itself lays Chicago's social stratification bare: "Between the girls in their sleazy silk stockings and the mothers in their shapeless shawls lay the rotten root of the trouble. New America and the Old World, out of sympathy with each other, uncomprehending, resentful . . . the shawled and formless older women stood or sat animal-like" (191). The "rotten root" is the inability to grown and change. Those who have not quite become Americans yet remain un-evolved, classified as "animal-like," "shapeless," and "formless." These descriptors suggest that until immigrants embrace American culture, including its clothing, they are not human.

Jennie wants to leave this formlessness associated with the Old World behind. "Jennie, the grub, [was] vainly trying to transform herself into Jeannette the butterfly" (193), writes Ferber. The process is difficult—for example, Jeannette attempts to emulate her American-born counterparts by bobbing her hair, but "[t]he style went oddly with the high-cheek-boned Slavic face, the blunt-fingered factory hands" (195). Mutation is a lengthy and vexed process, so that the immigrant cannot seamlessly become American, like the Thrifts, but must hack her way to assimilation with haircuts and "vain" tries at self-betterment. To provide the starkest contrast, on Lottie's young niece Charley, the same bobbed hairstyle is depicted as appealing and stylish, while Jeannette's remains incongruous.

In another coincidence harking back to Ferber's beloved Dickens, Charley falls in love with Jesse Dick the poet, descendant of the Jesse Dick who courted her Great-Aunt Charlotte. Charley categorizes Jesse's family as "'Holland Dutch,' I guess" (162), granting even her fellow-American companion an "other" heritage, even as her grandmother disapproves of Jesse Dick because he is a "butcher's boy" (264). Jesse is a poet who writes "'virile and American'" (244) depictions of Chicago, providing an interior literary reflection within *The Girls*. Ferber writes of Jesse's audience

> Perhaps they had just been reading the thing he called "Halsted Street." You know it:

> > Halsted Street. All the nations of the world.
> > Mill end sales; shlag stores; Polack women gossiping
> > Look at the picture of the bride in her borrowed wedding dress
> > Outside the Italian photograph gallery. (244)

Since Jesse Dick is a fictional character, this is, of course, Ferber's poetry, revealing the same crowded, heterogeneous type of urban environment that inspires Fanny to sketch. "All the nations" render the city vibrant, and in *The Girls*, many of these "nations" are at least mentioned in passing. With her "you know it," it is as if the reader, too, lives in the fictional world invented for *The Girls*. Ferber implicates her audience in her vision as well as in her characters' colorful, tense universe, lending some responsibility to the understanding of this time and place in which ethnic concerns prevail and make for continual anxiety.

Lottie's romance progresses without the thrills of her niece's (or her great-aunt's), although the two do, predictably, intersect. When she stops with her date, an oafish man named Ben Gartz, at the Dick family delicatessen, she is "conscious of a little shock. Immediately she was ashamed that this should be so" (247). Lottie cannot ignore the influence of the Dicks, and moves through the entire reaction—consciousness to shock to shame—rapidly when confronted with their store. She settles on being "ashamed," and although Lottie flirts with family disapproval by seeing Ford as a young girl, she internalizes the reaction enough to look down upon a working-class beau—this most recent Dick—for Charley. Invoking precedent, in the form of occupation rather than ethnicity, Jesse tells Gartz that "'I know of quite a good poet who was apprenticed to a butcher. . . . Shakespeare, his name was. Will Shakespeare'" (252). In likening himself to Shakespeare, Jesse defends himself with literary history, just his ancestor defends himself to a Thrift by reminding his girlfriend that his forbears came to New York with Hudson.

None of these connections can salvage the Dicks' standing as lower class, but the arrival of the First World War upends the Girls' world, both personally and culturally. Even more than the already accelerated American social ladder, the war overturns prescribed norms. The rescued Slav servant Jeanette remains a "grub" until the war Americanizes her. Submerged in American culture, she dances with "boys from Texas and boys from Massachusetts; boys from Arizona and Kansas and Ohio and Washington," and eventually marries one from Nebraska, completing her assimilation into American society and separating from her lower-class family for good (296). Her haircut no longer curtails her; married to a soldier, she becomes a full-fledged American. The war also provokes further ethnic stratification in Chicago, unnerving the war profiteer Ben Gartz. He says, "'now that they've brought all these niggers up from the South to work over at the Yards since the war it isn't fit to live in, that's what. Why, look at Grand Boulevard! Black up to Forty-Third Street. All those old houses. It's a shame!'" (285). Those "old houses" on the South side are like the Girls' house, as the novel demonstrates the ways in which a city's social lines can shift, turning an upper-class mansion into part of a more diverse neighborhood that a racist claims as unfit. Chicago continues to mutate, looking toward a world in which the lines crossed by Ford or the Dick family stand as precedents. With its hectic social pace only hastening, Chicago proves itself to be as malleable a character as Jeanette herself.

The war gives Lottie Thrift an excuse to leave Chicago and have her own adventures at last, and she heads to France to nurse soldiers. Charley, having heard that her aunt is tending a war orphan, writes, "'Send me a picture, won't you? I hope she isn't one of those awfully brune French babies that look a mixture of Italian and Yiddish and Creole'" (342). Ferber positions Charley as the young forward-thinker with her bobbed hair

and delicatessen-worker Dick boyfriend, but her bigotry runs just as deep
as that of the loutish Ben Gartz. Charley, who has clearly internalized
the Thrift racial superiority, is repelled by the idea of a non-white baby.
Selecting identities that can encourage passing for white heightens the
racial anxiety: the child might not be white, and Charley would not know
it. ("Yiddish" is, of course, a language, not an ethnonym, but Charley's
meaning is clear: she hopes the baby does not "look Jewish.") A friend sees
the baby in France and, relieved, reports that the baby is fair-complected:
"'they're not all dark, you know'" (354). Upon her return, the baby cries
and Carrie Payson says, "'Don't you think for one minute I'm going to
have any foreign baby screaming around this house'" (361).

The image of the baby as potentially "brune" masks the true illicit-
ness of her existence as the product of Lottie's brief alliance with a conve-
niently dead soldier. After years of repression concerning whom she can
date, Lottie has performed an act possibly even more shameful than dat-
ing a Jew: bearing a baby out of wedlock. Despite her illegitimate birth,
given her origins, Claire (named after the French word light, as if forever holding the shadow of darker skin at bay) is destined to be a future
Girl. Instead of advising Lottie to tell the truth about her daughter's background, however, the knowing Aunt Charlotte says: "'It's a brave lie, Lottie. You stick to it, for her. A topsy-turvy world she's come into. Perhaps
she'll be the one to work out what we haven't done—we Thrift girls'"
(274). The novel has taken place entirely in this "topsy-turvy" world
in the sense that the Thrift "girls," one after another, tended to reverse
course by refusing the people for whom they believed themselves destined. Hiding Claire's disreputable beginnings seems, in fact, to be what
"we Thrift girls" have already done, in that it simultaneously refutes and
reinstates the problems of American society, which are at the same time
so freeing—Lottie experiences a passionate love affair and bears the beloved daughter she desires—and restrictive—she will lie about her own
child. Even after the war and the wearing respectability of history, these
Girls remain grubs, waiting for their chances to become butterflies, while
the relentlessly changing city churns on around them.

During the mid-twenties, Ferber gave plenty of thought to young urban women like Charley and Jeanette, codified in a personality she called
the "the girl of today" and discussed in a 1924 interview with R. Heylbut

Wollstein for the *New York Times*. "She's a pretty ticklish proposition to talk about, this up-to-the-minute girl," Ferber said. "When she does do something, she knows why, and she's willing to take the consequences. Which, up to recently enough, was considered a distinctly masculine attribute. That's why I like her" (1924, 12). This emblematizes the concerns with which Ferber grappled as she worked. Ferber's novels are preoccupied with boundaries, translating here to the "up-to-the-minute girl" being considered masculine rather than feminine. Most saliently, this "girl" ends up likable, by Ferber's standards. Ferber's navigation of these parameters connects *The Girls* and *So Big*, for in many ways, the women in these two novels are moving from within their prescribed confines to confront those boundaries, which often put pressure upon ethnic concerns as well as gender ones. The "girl" Ferber mentions in the interview is in transition from the multiple Charlottes of *The Girls* to Selina, the protagonist of *So Big*.

Like *The Girls*, *So Big*, published in 1924, also concerns the transformation of a Chicago grub. Ferber had been thinking about the plot for five years, she said, but worried no one else would be interested in a "novel about a middle-aged woman in a calico dress and with wispy hair and bad teeth, grubbing on a little truck farm south of Chicago" (Dickinson 1925, 28). But with its extraordinary success—bestseller lists and a Pulitzer Prize—Ferber said, "I knew how the ugly duckling felt who turned into a swan" (Dickinson 1925, 29).

The book's wide appeal stems from its mixture of Horatio Alger–worthy transformations, which here elevate hard work instead of simple fortune as a motivating principle. Its heroine, Selina Peake DeJong, enjoys a privileged upbringing, but falls on hard times and, on a lark borne of desperation, marries a Dutch farmer. Through her toil-filled life she persists in worshipping beauty, and her own rarefied background combines with the Dutch rural life around her for a complex rumination on art, class, and ethnicity. The tensions between urban and rural, recent immigrant and long-standing resident, and agriculture and manufacturing all propel Selina's American story, in which ethnicities continue to proliferate as Ferber grapples with the ways in which America was growing and changing.

Selina, like the Thrift-Payson women, is a descendant of New England aristocrats—the Vermont Peakes—who falls into poverty after her dissolute father dies, leaving his daughter with his motto that life is a "fine show. The trick is to play in it and look at it at the same time" (1924, 13). Selina's doubled understanding, emblematized in this motto, along with her appreciation of beauty, helps her survive the change in circumstance as well as form her dreams for her son, Dirk. As *The Girls* does, *So Big* demonstrates the mercurial nature of the American social scale. As Ferber writes, echoing her own firefighter-to-operagoer hierarchy from *The Girls*, "in Chicago the distance from butcher of 1885 to packer of 1890 was only a five-year leap" (12).

The city of Chicago provides ethnic diversity as well as various financial strata. Selina lives an urban life, exposed to widely varied ethnicities, and Ferber fuses this experience with performance, the lens through which she herself saw the world as a theater-loving child. Like the young Ferber, Selina adores staged entertainment: "Selina, half-hidden in the depths of an orchestra seat, wriggled in ecstatic anticipation when the curtain ascended on the grotesque rows of Haverly's minstrels. . . . She witnessed that startling innovation, a Jewish play, called Samuel of Posen" (13). These diverse ethnic images, all historical figures—Haverly was a producer who hired both blackface minstrels and actual African American minstrels—and *Samuel of Posen*, a play about a Jewish peddler who vindicates some gentile friends—highlight Chicago's diversity and the world in which Selina learns to be an observer, whether in an orchestra seat or "witnessing" a play. Ethnic groups are ranged before Selina to be viewed, teaching her about different types of people through classification and display. Indeed, the process of categorizing people preoccupies Simeon Peake. "'There are only two kinds of people in the world that really count,'" he tells Selina. "'One kind's wheat, and the other kind's emeralds,'" he says, a rubric that provides Selina with a lifelong template for viewing people as types (13).

Chicago educates Selina, but after her father dies, she becomes submerged into the culture of the Dutch farmer, presented through a series of events as the only choice for her future besides throwing herself upon the mercy of her father's spinster sisters in Vermont, a pair of women she sees as "dried apple[s], with black fuzz and mould at [the] heart" (16). To avoid the New Englanders' distasteful company and moribund fate, Selina takes a job teaching school in High Prairie, the Dutch district southwest of Chicago. In contrast to the diverse ethnography of Chicago, High Prairie is a place where those who differ from their Dutch American neighbors—like Selina—are thrown into high relief. Selina instantly gains local (and mocking) fame among High Prairie's villagers by exclaiming over the beauty of the surrounding fields. Her urbane aesthetic appreciation sets her apart from her neighbors, as Ferber parses the stereotype of Dutch people as thrifty and hardworking into a lack of appreciation for beauty. Selina fancifully imagines that High Prairie farmers will resemble the "apple-cheeked" townsfolk in a Washington Irving story, asking one, "'How did you leave Rip?'" (34). Instead, however, she finds the locals concerned with cooking and farming, unwilling to indulge her artistic impulses. The Pools' eldest son, Roelf, offers her an exception. "The boy is, somehow, foreign looking—Italian," Selina notices (37). "Some Dutch sailor ancestor, Selina thought, or fisherman, must have touched at an Italian port or Spanish and brought back a wife whose eyes and skin and feeling for beauty had skipped layer on layer of placid Netherlanders to crop out now in this wistful sensitive boy" (47). In the country, where Selina longs for Chicago's ethnically variegated neighborhoods, Roelf's "foreign-looking" complexion renders him sympathetic to Selina, and they form a sympathetic pair of dark-haired aesthetes. For Ferber, some measure of refined foreignness helps when endeavoring to understand sophisticated concepts like art or beauty.

Selina's marriage to Pervus DeJong, a boilerplate example of the local Dutch farmers whose affection for her—and extreme handsomeness—marks his only deviation from the other farmers in High Prairie, does not hasten her assimilation. He promptly dies, and their son Dirk (the novel's name comes from his childhood nickname of Sobig) inherits his mother's aristocratic mien with his "slightly aquiline nose, probably a long-jump inheritance from some Cromwellian rapscallion of the English Peakes of a past century" (107). Selina's higher-class attitudes are internally manifest to the point that they leave an imprint on her son, further distancing them from the rest of the locals. Further, she takes on the traditionally male job of traveling to Chicago to the Haymarket, where farmers sell produce. She tells Dirk that, as in the *Arabian Nights*, "'All kinds of things can happen. All kinds of people . . . Caliphs, and princes, and slaves, and thieves, and good fairies, and witches'" (123).

Selina leans on her own understanding of a framework of literary culture and imagery, but in this case applies to real-life heterogeneity. Her fantastic categories translate into the ethnic identities that await in the city and extends to the diverse (and typically more prosaically classified) ethnic types that populate the farmer's market: "Peddlers and small grocers swarmed in at four—Greeks, Italians, Jews. They bought shrewdly, craftily, often dishonestly. They sold their wares to the housewives. Their tricks were many. . . . A swarthy face had Luigi, a swift brilliant smile, a crafty eye. . . . Stolid red Dutch faces, sunburned. Lean dark foreign faces. Shouting, clatter, turmoil" (135). These ethnic "others" form a sort of predatory group around the Dutch farmers at the market. For all Selina's description of Ali Baba's riches, she seems more to have fallen in with the Forty Thieves.

As in *The Girls,* Chicago alters daily. The demographics of Selina's home city shift under her gaze: "Yankee names they used to be. Flint-Keen-Rusk-Lane. Now you saw Cuneo-Meleges-Campagna" (137). Change and growth represent the sort of urban dynamism Selina has missed while in High Prairie, but also distorts her original vision of the city. Her own "Yankee" maiden name—Peake—would have fit right in on one of the old signs, but now seems incongruous next to the new ones, so that she is less a creature of the Arabian Nights than a reader. A different mythology follows Selina when she and Dirk, penniless, must spend the night in their own wagon, "[m]uch like another woman who had laid in the straw with her child in her arms almost two thousand years before" (132). As Selina morphs into the Virgin Mary, Ferber's use of history leaps past Selina's New England origins to ally her with Christian beginnings. The heterogeneous and urban market gives way to one association for Selina, as she becomes as pure as Mary, lying in a wagon.

The city does offer Selina salvation in the form of a Dutch meat tycoon, suggesting that life after Dutch culture can offer a family financial and social success. Selina reunites with her friend Julie, whose father, Aug Hempel, has achieved both types of success with the speed Ferber mentions at the start of the novel. Having ascended from being a butcher to a pork magnate, Aug has assimilated thoroughly to the point that he "talked almost without an accent; used the idiomatic American speech he heard about the yards" (149). Although upper class, Aug uses lower-class lingo to fit in. Aug loans Selina money, and, having fallen due to her own father's dissolution, Selina achieves social ascendancy for herself and Dirk through his largesse. Hempel's faith and investment are repaid when she succeeds, and her "output was sought a year in advance by the South Water Street commission merchants. DeJong asparagus with firm white thick stalk bases tapering to a rich green streaked with lavender at the tips" (156). Evocative of today's gastronomical preoccupation with produce's origins on restaurant menus, and mimicking, to a lesser extent, the ascent of Aug Hempel, Selina manages to marry her aesthetic desires (the "lavender asparagus") with her financial needs. She has made the fields beautiful in her own way, and feeds not only her family but her city on the jewel-like edible proceeds.

During the *So Big* period, Ruth Brindze wrote a profile of Ferber as a winning and almost elfin woman—"Her eyes are dark and sparkling and her mouth has a way of always turning up at the corners into a smile"— that recalls Selena's dedication to the validating quality of labor: "When she is writing fiction she does not wait for inspiration. . . . She goes out and meets inspiration nine-tenths of the way. . . . Edna Ferber is a thoroughly businesslike young woman. She has so much work to do and she does it. She doesn't wait for inspiration. She doesn't wait for anything else. The work gets finished on time" (1924). Ferber's own love for aesthetic perfection was necessarily put aside so that she could continue to make money from her writing, and support her mother and sister that way. Like Selina, Ferber worked for her own livelihood while integrating her artistic interest when she could.

Dirk, Selina's son, lists too far in his own balance, becoming too "thoroughly businesslike" to succeed within his mother's—and Ferber's— criteria of earning a good living while maintaining an investment in cultural betterment. At college in Chicago, Dirk, following in his mother's footsteps of appreciating difference, befriends an "Unclassified," student, a 38-year-old woman named "Schwengauer. Mattie Schwengauer— terrible!" (*So Big* [1924], 166). The disharmonious name signals a somehow troublesome ethnicity. But Dirk, preferring to meld into the higher social classes than embrace this immigrant, drops Mattie because his fraternity brothers disapprove of her. Selina, crushed, says, "'But this Mattie—why, she's life. Do you remember the story of when she washed dishes in the kosher restaurant over on Twelfth Street and the proprietor used to rent out dishes and cutlery for Irish and Italian neighborhood weddings where they had pork and goodness knows what all, and then use them next day in the restaurant again for the kosher customers?'" (170). This vaguely anti-Semitic anecdote, with the presumably Jewish owners of a kosher restaurant duping their co-religionists and disrespecting their religious training to earn extra money, seems an odd choice to illustrate a character's vibrancy. Nevertheless, it falls into the category of praising Mattie, who clearly recognizes the same urban dynamics that Selina appreciates and believes constitute an understanding of a well-lived life. Her heterogeneity, including a life replete with Jewish, Irish, and Italian figures, in Selina's formulation, is "life."

Dismissing Mattie is only the first blot on the escutcheon of Dirk's reputation and his mother's approval. While he is an architect, a profession in line with Selina's faith in the importance of aesthetics, he also falls in love with Aug Hempel's granddaughter Paula, a materialistic girl who candidly announces that she wants to marry someone richer. Spurred by this rejection, he turns to finance and grows wealthy, employing a dialect-speaking Japanese butler, referred to as "the Jap" (218, 254). Dirk shows his wealth in other ways: "He learned to call it 'running over to Europe for a few days.' It had all come about in a scant two years, as is the theatrical way in which life speeds in America" (205). Dirk achieves the American dream—firefighter to operagoer—while bypassing the appreciation of beauty that his mother so values and the understanding of a hard day's labor that Aug Hempel accumulates. Dirk is neither emeralds nor wheat, making him a disappointment to his mother, the one person who somehow—the theater, asparagus—manages to embody both.

Unlike Dirk, Roelf Pool successfully collides images of ethnicity with the themes of aesthetic appreciation. Roelf—Selina's emerald to Aug Hempel's wheat—befriends Dallas O'Mara, an artist of Dirk's age whom Dirk adores. These two aesthetes, one representing Selina's generation and one representing Dirk's, reappear late in the novel, dei ex machina who point up Dirk's failure to prize beauty over commerce, but nevertheless play a crucial role in sketching Ferber's framework of the ways in which ethnicities intersect in America, both through anxiety and necessity.

Dallas, with her brash and hyper-American first name and Irish surname, embraces heterogeneity and urban life, just like Selina. Her associates, including Dirk, are wide-ranging in both race and class. They share
a passion for the arts, demonstrating anew that Dirk, despite his archi-
tectural training, evades both ethnic richness and artistic enlightenment.
One passage in particular highlights the ways in which the character of
Dallas brings to light the ethnic unease and stratification that character-
izes Chicago and, in turn, America. In Dallas's studio, "[a] swarthy foreign-
looking chap . . . was playing softly at the piano" (230). This man,
"swarthy" and artistic like *The Girls'* Jewish writer Ford and *Fanny Herself*'s Jewish artist Fanny, is a thinly disguised (his name is Bert Colson) Al
Jolson. He and Dallas perform for the others in the studio:

> Colson sang those terrible songs about April showers bringing violets,
> and about mah Ma-ha-ha-ha-ha-ha-ha-my but they didn't seem terrible
> when he sang them. There was about this lean, hollow-chested, som-
> ber-eyed comedian a poignant pathos, a gorgeous sense of rhythm—a
> something unnameable that bound you to him, made you love him. . . .
> He talked like a bootblack and sang like an angel. Dallas at the piano,
> he leaning over it, were doing "blues." The two were rapt, ecstatic. I
> got the blues—I said the blues—I got the this or that—the somethin-
> gorother—blue-hoo hoos. . . . Colson sang the cheaply sentimental
> ballad as though it were the folk-song of a tragic race. His arms were
> extended, his face rapt. As Dallas played the tears stood in her eyes.
> (232)

The beginning of this passage refers to two of Al Jolson's best-known
songs, "April Showers," in which he sings: "So if it's raining, have no regrets / Because it isn't raining rain, you know / It's raining violets," and
"Swanee River," in which he sings about his "Mammy." Jolson, of course,
was Jewish—the son of a cantor who became famous partially due to his
blackface singing of such standards. The idea of the blues as performed
by a Jewish blackface performer rather than an African American adds
to the image of Chicago as a "fine show." Any blackface performer is a
troubled and troubling observer of another culture, as Eric Lott argues
when he writes that minstrelsy is "the dialectical flickering of racial in-

sult and racial envy" (1995, 18). Dallas and Bert exemplify this with their song, which comforts listeners even though it is "cheaply sentimental," as Ferber writes. The song might sound like "the folk-song of a tragic race," if it is standard minstrel fare, but could also refer to Colson's Jewishness, which, as Fanny's character demonstrates, Ferber often couches in terms of tragedy or suffering. The drama of the moment—enough to make Dallas weep—only adds to its import, while Dirk's exclusion from these proceedings—further complicated and more deeply felt when he finds out that Dallas wrote the song—demonstrates his inability to understand art. His shortcomings reveal themselves as Dallas emerges as a protean image of the perfect American artist, the exact person his mother sacrificed for him to become even as he rejected her plans for him. As Dirk thinks: "This was one Dallas. There were a dozen—a hundred. Yet she was always the same." (1924, 234).

Dirk's failure is complete. Roelf and Selina reunite, and Ferber writes, "It was as though he were her one son, and had come home" (251). Selina's one son has, in fact, come home, and does so all the time, but those reunions are far less rewarding, since Dirk stays linked to finance rather than art, to shallow Paula rather than vibrant Dallas or even the earthy Mattie Schwengauer. Dallas decides she wants to paint Selina because she is "distinguishedly American . . . the jaw-line like that of the women who came over in the Mayflower; or crossed the continent in a covered wagon" (251). The image of Selina as an ultimate representative of American history—Mayflower, covered wagon—leaves Dirk adrift. Without ties to agriculture or art, and with any trace of his Dutch identity washed away, Dirk is doomed to soullessness. Chicago provides his only interest, and Dirk compares the vital and unreachable Dallas to the city itself, since both are a "mixture of grandeur and cheapness; of tawdriness and magnificence; of splendour and ugliness" (239).

This "mixture," attributed to the city itself, also speaks to Ferber's themes in these two novels. The idea of difference and intersecting identities emerges in *The Girls* and *So Big*, prefiguring treatises of mixture like *Cimarron* and *Giant*. The city foments ethnicity and class collisions that shape individuals and communities, and these textured narrative moments demonstrate Ferber's understanding of the relentless mixture America foments, which benefits those—Dallas, Ford, Jesse Dick,

Selina—who appreciate it. The complex confines and characters of the Windy City would return in Ferber's next work, but only after a lengthy sojourn on the similarly oxymoronically freeing and confining Mississippi River in the 1926 *Show Boat*. In these books, the inclinations remain tendentious—Ford's rejection, Dirk's isolation—but begin the work of impressing the notion of mixture as inevitably American. *So Big* and *The Girls* demonstrate the inevitable blurring of categories that an ever-evolving America offers, and Ferber would next begin to look toward a society in which those combinations work their way in from the margins.

3

A PINPRICK OF BLOOD
Show Boat

OF ALL OF FERBER'S NOVELS, the 1926 novel *Show Boat* may be the most difficult to separate from the subsequent artistic works that have come to be associated with it, from the iconic ballad "Ol' Man River" to the elaborate dance numbers in the 1951 film version to the unceasing restagings at community theaters and summer stocks across the country. The same is true within literary criticism. Because of its treatment of many issues pertinent to American literature in general—racial tension and passing among them—critics have considered *Show Boat* alongside texts ranging from Frances Harper's 1892 *Iola LeRoy* to Nella Larsen's 1929 *Passing* to Mark Twain's 1885 *Huckleberry Finn*. Due to these various iterations and treatments, *Show Boat* has probably left the widest track on the American imagination of all of Ferber's novels. In fact, Lauren Berlant terms *Show Boat* a "supertext" because of these multiple versions (2008, 75).

In an article about *Show Boat*, the famously workmanlike Ferber said that writing the novel "was the nearest I ever came to enjoyment of my particular craft" ("My Son, The Show Boat" [1966], 172). She had heard about showboats from a theater colleague, and she grew entranced with the idea of waterborne performance. She headed to North Carolina to spend some time on *The James Adams Floating Theatre*, a showboat owned by Charles and Beulah Hunter. The Hunters were self-proclaimed fans of Ferber's—they loved her Emma McChesney stories—and welcomed her aboard. Ferber met up with the Hunters in Bath, North Carolina, one April, reveling in the Pamlico River scene and taking plenty of notes. She stayed on the boat for a few days and wrote the book in Paris and New York. The resulting work, *Show Boat*, was serialized in *Woman's Home Companion* in 1926, and then published as a novel.

In his review of the novel in the *Brooklyn Daily Eagle*, George Currie writes, "The scene to her [Ferber] is no less important than the story, and the story is on a par with her ideas. She has a knack of making her book read like a story, which is what most readers ask. At the same time, she does not pander to the fugitive delights of the book stall mob" (1926). Long before the term "middlebrow" was applied to Ferber by literary scholars, her contemporary critics saw the same qualities of large ideas writ accessible in her work. "She does not believe that all the changes are improvements, and is not afraid to say so. . . . She has said a number of things that need saying, and that make good reading," wrote an anonymous *Rochester Democrat* reviewer in an article called "Where Life Is All Drama (1926, 19). Audiences appreciated not only Ferber's large topics, but also the way in which her grand plots buoyed them along. With the approval of her masses and the ready stage machine, the *Show Boat* industry took off in 1927, when the musical version premiered on Broadway. It has not stopped since.

Even Ferber herself played with *Show Boat's* extraordinary fame in her 1958 novel *Ice Palace*, emphasizing the cosmopolitan nature of a town in Alaska by writing that nightclub singers there choose to sing "Ol' Man River." Too, she personally enjoyed the effects of the supertext: "I must break down and confess to being one of those whose eyes grow dreamy and whose mouth is wreathed in wistful smiles whenever the orchestra— any orchestra—plays Ol' Man River" (*A Peculiar Treasure* [1939], 271). She thought of her works as children, and that "[o]ne in particular, conceived in an idle moment, turned out to be a source of seemingly inexhaustible comfort and exhilaration to his Ma. If ever he caused a moment's unhappiness it is now forgotten, like measles in childhood. His name is Show Boat" ("My Son, The Show Boat" [1966], 73).

Even with all the attention to the general *Show Boat* topic, an article in the *Washington Post* highlights the importance of considering novel and play separately. The piece documents a new production, which theatergoers mockingly referred to as "No Boat" because of its minimalist staging. As choreographer Karma Camp was quoted by Celia Wren in the *Washington Post*, "'Some people think, "Show Boat!" I can't wait to see it! The singing and the dancing! It's such a great, fun show!'" Hearing such reactions, she added, she is tempted to reply, "'Fun? Oh, my gosh, it's actually horrendous what happens in it!'" (2009, E4).

Anyone familiar with the novel would know that already. Reading Ferber's text yields right away the complex racial themes and politics to which Camp and Schaeffer respond. Minus stage dressing, musical numbers, or visual panoramas of the Mississippi, *Show Boat* navigates vexed discussions on ethnicity, passing, and bigotry. It includes violence and racism. Stereotypes circulate around the character of Julie, a half–African American actress passing for white on a boat traveling the Mississippi, a symbol of the fluid spaces of Ferber's vision of American society. The novel strives for an accurate portrayal of a slim, adrift slice of the American theater. (At one point, it actually seemed *too* accurate—a gambler named Tom Taggart sued Doubleday for allowing Ferber to use his real name in the book. Taggart won, and subsequent editions were scrubbed.)

Show Boat stands at the center of Ferber's process of understanding and writing about ethnic mixture and its relevance. Where *The Girls* and *So Big* delved into the notion of mixture as it concerns white ethnicity, with *Show Boat* Ferber broached the topic of racism and racial mixing which would motivate later novels such as *Cimarron, Saratoga Trunk*, and *Giant*. Yet *Show Boat* does not offer as much of the equation of mixture equaling strength that arrives with those later works. For one thing, Ferber was still grappling with her own issues of cultural construction of race and difference, and the novel contains toxic slurs referring to African Americans as well as more generic racial categorization. It showcases a significant moment for Ferber. The character of Julie, around whom the mixture plot circulates, is not a melting-pot heroine but instead falls under the nineteenth- and early twentieth-century American literary rubric of tragic mulatta—in which a mixed-race woman, often attempting to pass for white, meets a troubled end. Yet it is Magnolia, the white daughter of the showboat captain, who, despite the lily-white associations of her southern and arboreally inspired name, draws upon her association with African Americans—including, most crucially, the African American Julie—and the very slight suggestion that she may be of mixed race herself to succeed and thrive.

"Culture requires social space, institutional settings, for its enactment and reproduction," writes Michael Walzer (1998, 88). In other words, culture needs performance to move forward, and *Show Boat* provides the framing for cultural production. Its internal emphasis is on the stage, and Ferber adds a more outward-looking focus on racial questions with its plot. While much of *Show Boat*'s complexity grows out of the tragic-mulatta narrative, it also represents a rewriting of it in many ways. As Juda Bennett writes, "Julie's story of racial 'passing' structures the rest of the narrative, and . . . bleeds through into Magnolia's story" (1996, 75).

Although the crux of the novel's racial tensions circulates around Julie and Magnolia, the *Cotton Blossom*'s captain, Andy Hawks, is also presented as possessing ethnic difference. Ferber identifies Captain Andy with a far-flung ethnic identity—Basque—and he slightly resembles *So Big*'s Roelf Pool, whose dark hair and eyes are also attributed to Spanish genetics from a distant ancestor. Andy says that "[h]is real name was André and . . . he was descended, through his mother, from a long line of Basque fisher-folk. . . . It probably was true, and certainly accounted for his swarthy skin, his bright brown eyes, his impulsiveness, his vivacious manner" (1926, 21). Andy's "swarthiness" recalls that of the Jewish Ford in *The Girls*, but the way in which he associates his coloring with a romantic, pastoral European heritage keeps him from being cast as racially different in an American context. The novel, however, uses this "Basque past" to emphasize Captain Andy's current sympathy with his African American employees.

At one point, Andy's shrill and domineering wife, New Englander Parthy Ann, rails against an African American cook, who she believes is wasting food. Angered by her presumption, the cook hurls the garbage at her, saying "[t]hey's something for you take to the Captain to show him, missy'" (24). While Andy does dismiss the cook after the incident, "something round and gleaming was seen to pass from the Captain's hairy little brown hand to the big black paw" (25). The association between the characters is clear, with the "hairy little brown hand" as inhuman as the "black paw." Both are animals. With his questionably "Basque" heritage, Captain Andy is clearly of the "brune" variety of European lamented by Charley in *The Girls*, and thus more akin to his employees than his wife.

Andy and Parthy Ann's daughter, Magnolia, exists at the crossroads of her parents' ethnic identities. Ferber writes that the showboat surroundings were "all, perhaps, the worst possible environment for a skinny, high-strung, and sensitive little girl who was one-quarter French. But Magnolia thrived on it. She had the solid and lumpy Puritanism of Parthy's presence to counteract the leaven of her volatile father. This saved her from being utterly consumed" (1926, 65). Here Andy's ancestry slips from being "possibly" true to a vital part of his daughter's identity: Magnolia is "one-quarter French." Like the autobiographical "oriental" Fanny, Magnolia is also "high-strung." Ferber uses a culinary metaphor to explain Magnolia's personality and heritage through likening her parents to whiter-than-white flour and brown, activating yeast, which, of course, produces the nourishing combination of bread. Magnolia is, as Ferber writes, "all Andy—manner, temperament, coloring" (22). Andy passes on all of his vibrant personality traits along with his dark complexion, which causes Parthy to admonish Magonia to wear a sun hat since she is "black enough as 'tis" (88). African Americanness is a constant theme, whether it comes up with through Parthy Ann's racism or Julie and Andy's vexed sympathies and personal affiliations.

Besides the light-brown complexion of all three, Andy and Magnolia share affection and respect for Julie, a talented actress who performs on the showboat. Magnolia notices that Julie's eyes are "deep, and dark, and dead. . . . The veil wound round her bonnet hung down her back, imparting a Spanish and mysterious look" (41). Between mentions of being "Basque" and "Spanish," Julie and Andy are similarly coded, suggesting a community of non-whiteness between them. Julie's secret—her African American heritage—is foretold in the repeated physical description of her eyes, "deep-set and really black, and there was about them a curious indefinable quality. . . . [Magnolia thinks that] [h]er own eyes were dark, but not like Julie's. Perhaps it was the whites of Julie's eyes that were different" (69). This passage's preoccupation with the extremes of white and black, defined by clear physical markers, demonstrates that Julie's whiteness marks her as different to the very sclera of her eyes, a physical characteristic that is typically unquestionably white in every healthy person. This "indefinable quality" serves to heighten the mystery in Julie's background and increases the motivation to learn what she is hiding.

This secrecy is a direct inheritor of the literary tragic-mulatta plot in American literature. As Carla Peterson defines this trope, it "centers on a

beautiful fair-skinned girl . . . who remains ignorant of her slave identity.
. . . At the moment of narrative crisis, her slave condition is discovered,
or remembered, and she is remanded into slavery" (1995, 154). Often,
death—usually dramatic and unexpected—follows.[1] While Julie is not a
slave, her identity in the Jim Crow South makes her a target for racism
and abuse, and provides the reason she left the South for an itinerant life
on the showboat in the first place. Julie—and her white husband Steve—
guard her secret, but the threat of discovery haunts her, and a trajectory
similar to the tragic mulatta awaits. *Show Boat* is not a direct translation
of the tradition but contains enough of its key elements to form a commentary upon it.

Julie's identity as an actress adds layers to the performative aspect of
her life and her character—a crucial portion of being a tragic mulatta—
as well as incorporating the transformative nature of theater, not just for
the performers but for the audience as well. During performances on the
Cotton Blossom, racial arrangement expands and infuses the scene to the
point that variously raced images of people morph into those of magical
beings, recalling Selina's description of the farmers' market in *So Big* as a
place with caliphs, fairies, and witches. Ferber writes that in the light of
the kerosene torches "[t]he whites of the Negroes' eyes gleamed whiter.
The lights turned their cheeks to copper and bronze and polished ebony.
The swarthy coal miners and their shawled and sallow wives, the farmers of the corn and wheat lands . . . the lovers two by two were magically
transformed into witches, giants, princesses, crones, gnomes, Nubians,
genii" (1926, 78). The condition of being in the audience renders the
spectators as transformed as the actors before them (the African American viewers, notably have "whiter" gleaming eyes, like Julie's), lending a
quality of melodrama to the situations unfolding within the *Cotton Blossom* as well as those performed on its stage.

Although she eventually is pressed into performing in these dramatic
scenes (both staged and real), Magnolia possesses an artistic skill different from Julie's. She learns songs from Jo and Queenie, two African

---

1. I've argued elsewhere that in her 1936 novel *Gone With the Wind*, Margaret Mitchell
uses the ingredients of the tragic-mulatta plot, including appearance, mixture and passing,
to encode Scarlett O'Hara as a foil to the tragic mulatta, since for the white Scarlett, her
Irish ethnicity brings her strength and success in the reconstructing South.

American employees on the boat, and copies them. "Unconsciously, being an excellent mimic, she sang as Jo and Queenie sang, her head thrown slightly back, her eyes rolling or half closed. . . . [S]he got into this the hoarsely sweet Negro overtone—purple velvet muffling a flute," Ferber writes (92). Her mother is appalled by her daughter's affinity with the African American singers: "'White people aren't good enough for you, I suppose?'" she says (93). Parthy calls Julie "'that slatternly yellow cat,'" mingling color both with sexual availability and dehumanizing insult. This phrase also uses natural imagery to connect Julie to the Mississippi, variously termed a "tawny tigress," "big yella snake," with "golden yellow skin" (88, 9, 11, 10). Through Ferber's characteristically strong imagery, both Julie and the river are encoded in ways that are natural and powerful.

In much the same way that she elides Julie with nature through the river and animals, Ferber emphasizes the importance of the African American musicians' influence on Magnolia. Of Jo, she writes that his "feeling for time and beat and measure and pitch was flawless. . . . Certainly Magnolia learned more of real music from black Jo and many another Negro wharf minstrel than she did from the heavy-handed and unlyrical George" (94). The contrast between the talented, albeit "charming and shiftless" Jo (90), whose job aboard the *Cotton Blossom* is in the kitchen, and the white music director, George, is patent and underscores the racist system under which the showboat travels. Jo may possess more talent, but he must work for George.

The crucible of the text surrounds the revelation of Julie's race and exposes that system. After the boat docks in the fictional town of LeMoyne, Mississippi, someone repeatedly steals Julie's publicity photograph. She takes to her bed, and her husband, a "blond giant" (103) named Steve, says that she will be well after leaving the town. Parthy recalls that Julie developed the same mysterious illness in the same town the year before, and it develops that Pete, a shady engineer with designs on Julie, exposes Julie and Steve's criminal miscegenation. Once Pete's betrayal is known, "[a] strange and terrible thing was happening. . . . Steve's eyes seemed suddenly to sink far back in his head. His cheek-bones showed gaunt and sharp as Julie's own" (108). Steve's "blond" appearance alters to resemble that of the African American Julie. Next, he acts to fulfill their sameness: "With incredible swiftness he seized Julie's hand in his left one and ran the keen glittering blade firmly across the tip of his forefinger. A scarlet line followed it. He bent his blond head, pressed his lips to the wound, sucked it greedily. . . . The scene was like a rehearsal of a *Cotton Blossom* thriller" (109). The self-conscious performative moment has twofold real roots: for one, Charles Hunter, the captain of the showboat Ferber spent time on, said that the incident actually happened, and that he knew the people involved. (Gilbert 1978, 380). The moment also resonates because it is a play within a play, with actors behaving dramatically, demonstrating the sheer melodrama of the racist, divisive laws of the contemporary South.

As the situation combusts within the novel, art and life continue to blend, down to the bigoted southern sheriff of whom Ferber writes, "Steve himself, made up for the part, couldn't have done it better" (1926, 109). This elision emphasizes Steve's racial identity as well as the collusion of drama and life; the person whom he most resembles—especially "made up for the part"—is his antagonist, not his wife. The ludicrousness of the "drop of blood" rule in the segregated South is demonstrated when Steve introduces a literal drop of Julie's blood into his own body. "'You wouldn't call a man a white man that's got Negro blood in him, would you?'" he asks the sheriff, who responds "'not in Mississippi'" (110). Since Julie is from LeMoyne, the sheriff knows her mixed background. "'I kind of smell a nigger in the woodpile here in more ways than one'" (113), he says, a gesture toward Steve's despondent act and his insistence that he is black.

Elly, a white woman who plays the boat's ingenue roles, peels back the curtain on the insubstantial world of the showboat by positioning herself against her colleague, demonstrating that not all the *Cotton Blossom*'s denizens are as righteous or quick to defend Julie and Steve from the sheriff as Captain Andy and Magnolia are. Instead, she threatens to quit if Julie does not leave immediately. "'She's black! She's black! God, I was a fool not to see it all the time. Look at her, the nasty yellow—' A stream of abuse, vile, obscene, born of the dregs of river talk heard through the years, now welled to Elly's lips, distorting them horribly" (114). Spewing racist vitriol physically alters Elly, arguing for the hideousness of bigotry and demonstrating a mutable and mask-like nature. Not only is Elly a racist, the revelation of her true self turns her into something "distorted," far more inhuman than the "nasty yellow" object of her insults. If Julie is the tawny yellow river, Elly is the "dregs." Her "performance" is no less dramatic than Steve's, in some ways, and proves the depths of feeling plumbed by Julie's decision to pass as well as turning the idea of the ingenue—young, delicate, innocent—entirely upside down with her ugly and jaded tirade.

After Julie's expulsion, Magnolia and Julie say goodbye with an embrace, "And when finally they came together . . . as you saw them sharply outlined against the sunset the black of the woman's dress and the white of the child's frock were as one" (116). This blatant image of opposites both cements the connection between Julie and Magnolia and demonstrates the instability of terms such as "white" and "black" when these definitions become indistinct merely through viewing them in silhouette. Black and white are, in Ferber's vision, "as one." Without Julie, Magnolia's identity continues to blend with hers. When she grows up and falls in love with a luckless gambler named Gaylord Ravenal, Magnolia's skin is "softly radiant as though lighted by an inner glow, as Julie's amber coloring, in the years gone by, had seemed to deepen into golden brilliance" (143). Even Gay's shady past—he killed a man in a gambling brawl—becomes linked with Julie's situation. Parthy yells, "'Who warned you about that yellow-skinned Julie! And what happened! If sheriffs is what you want, I'll wager you could get them fast enough if you spoke his name in certain parts of this country'" (145). In Parthy's formulation, having committed murder is the equivalent to being half African American, with both conditions counting as something shameful and worthy of persecution. Julie and Magnolia remain portions of one whole, the embodiment of women defying race conventions in a race-obsessed culture.

Ravenal offers a contrast to Magnolia because of his own patrician origins. Ravenel (spelled with an "e") is one of South Carolina's oldest white names, and by borrowing it for the Tennessee-born Ravenal, Ferber takes a short-cut to associations of Old South aristocracy. In order to prove his noble birth, Gay takes Andy and Magnolia to a graveyard in which Ravenals are buried. Also, he defends Magnolia by calling out a man who posts Magnolia's picture to warn others of the dangers of being an actress. The situation recalls and then inverts the traumatic drop-of-blood events unleashed by a photograph of Julie earlier in the novel, allying Magnolia with her childhood friend once again.

Also like Julie, Magnolia leaves the river for Chicago, where Magnolia and Gay interact within an intertextual moment: "the papers had been full of the shooting of Simeon Peake, the gambler. . . . Ravenal had known Simeon Peake," Ferber writes (185). Peake, of course, is Selina's father, the feckless cardsharp from Ferber's 1924 *So Big*. Using an event from another of her novels reveals the direness of Gay's future, as well as the hopelessness of Magnolia's. The gambling habits of Gay and Simeon provide an easy metaphor for the vicissitudes of rising and falling in station in America, as the couple vacillates between wealth and poverty. As with Simeon Peake, affection for the twin artifices of acting and gambling forces a downfall. Magnolia sustains herself through African American influence, distilled into lessons learned and tenderly remembered from Julie, Jo, and Queenie. "Kim Ravenal was probably the only white child north of the Mason and Dixon line who was sung to sleep to the tune of those plaintive, wistful, Negro plantation songs which were later to come into such vogue as spirituals. . . . Magnolia sang these songs, always, as she had learned to sing them in unconscious imitation of the soft husky Negro voice of her teacher" Ferber writes (221). In a reversal of Julie's fate, Magnolia even passes for black sight-unseen, impressing an African American audience. As she sings to her daughter in a hotel, "bell boys and waiters had eagerly gathered outside the closed door in what was, perhaps, as flattering and sincere a compliment as ever a singer received" (222). She receives her audience with "a little shriek of surprise and terror mingled" (222). Her African American audience frightens and shocks her, leaving open the question of whether she is more taken aback by her own ability to evoke emotion or because of being understood as African American herself. Also, the episode highlights the mercurial nature of passing, for just as Steve lays bare the ridiculousness of the "one-drop" rule, Magnolia's songs demonstrate the many ways in which Americans form racial assumptions—here, both visually and through auditory information.

More assumptions echo the question of passing when Gay takes Magnolia to a bachelor party at which the other guests' female escorts are prostitutes. Although others come to realize that Magnolia is not for hire, she does in fact end up performing for the audience of prostitutes and gamblers, mingling her past as a questionably reputed actress with their

roles as sexually available. Magnolia sings a song called "Deep River" she
learned from Jo and Queenie: "She swayed a little, gently. It was an unconscious imitation of old Jo's attitude" (243). A fellow gambler says, "I
never heard any song like *that* called a coon song," drawing the line already detailed in the Bert Colson—Al Jolson segment of *So Big* between
the upbeat "coon" songs made popular by minstrel shows and African
American spiritual music, and demonstrating Ferber's focus on what she
considered authentic expression (243).

Magnolia performs a spiritual called "All God's Chillun Got Wings,"
but refuses to sing a more rollicking song called "What! Marry Dat Gal."
As they leave, Magnolia tells Gay that the prostitutes of that night's party
are much like their audiences aboard the showboat. The bachelor party
becomes another instance of layered-over race, class, and performance,
throwing into relief the tensions between all three as Ferber puts forth
a society that is so far unwilling to countenance cultural mingling. According to the economy of the novel, which individual is "on stage" when
is no more than a matter of circumstance at any given moment, with
the prostitutes performing the role of party guests, and Magnolia for the
evening starring as a minstrel, co-opting Jo and Queenie's songs. As Bennett writes, "*Show Boat* takes the first step in removing the mask from
blackness by focusing its attention on the mask" (1996, 75), and it is this
mask that offers Magnolia security within this particular context. With
no relief from poverty in sight, Gay borrows money from a madam named
Hetty Chilson, or "ol' Het," as he calls her, indicating a familiarity between them that causes Magnolia to decide to return the money. Upon
seeing Hetty's butler, Mose, "Magnolia did not know why the sight of this
rather sad-eyed looking black man should have reassured her, but it did"
(1926, 265). Her affinity for anyone African American—even the very
tangential character Mose—comforts her even in the most dire situations. Mose literally opens a door for Magnolia, whose resolve in returning Gay's funds prompts new independence.

Mose proves only the briefest—if crucial—antecedent to Magnolia's
emboldening experiences with African American people. After Hetty and
Magnolia resolve their financial affairs, the women await Hetty's secretary to finalize the paperwork:

> Down this stair came a straight slim gray-haired figure. Genteel, was
> the word that popped into Magnolia's mind. A genteel figure in decent
> black silk, plain and good. It rustled discreetly. She paused a moment
> in the glow of the hall lamp as Hetty Chilson instructed her. A white
> face—no, not white—ivory. Like something dead. White hair still
> faintly streaked with black. . . . The eyes were incredibly bright in that
> ivory face; like dull coals, Magnolia thought, staring at her, fascinated.
> Something in her memory stirred at sight of this woman in the garb
> of a companion-secretary and with a face like burned out ashes. (268)

Everything about the "companion-secretary" is upright and sober, so that
instead of being illicitly coded in line with working in a house of prostitu-
tion, she is instead proper to a fault. This puritanical dress, however, does
not automatically disinclude Julie—whom Hetty calls "Jule"—from a life
of ill fame, since Hetty's "girls" are famous for wearing "rich, quiet, almost sedate clothes; and no paint on their faces" (209). Ferber leaves unclear whether Julie works as a prostitute or only as a secretary for Hetty,
and Steve's presumed absence from the scene is never explained. Nunlike
in her black dress, Julie appears aged with her white hair, which stands
in contrast to her skin, still emphatically not white but "ivory." Julie's appearance represents an extinguished life, as suggested by her "dull coals"
for eyes and "burned out ashes" of a face, harking back to how she looked
when Magnolia first saw her, with "deep, dark, and dead" eyes. There is
no future for the tragic mulatta, trapped in a house of ill repute, even
though she may not actually be a prostitute.

Further, the understanding that the secretary is actually Julie mutates
rapidly into a ghost story, as Magnolia "saw the smile of the woman [Julie]
freeze into a terrible contortion of horror. Horror stamped itself on her
every feature. Her eyes were wild and enormous with it; her mouth gaped
with it. . . . Then the woman turned and blindly vanished up the stairs
like a black ghost" (269). Magnolia imagines she has "seen the ghost of a
woman I knew when I was just a little girl" (269). This terror-filled moment—Julie metamorphosing from a person into some kind of specter—
propels Magnolia forward. She does not follow Julie, but neither does
she return to her old life or fashion herself as a victim of Gay. Instead,

she becomes the substantive figure opposing Julie's spectral one, taking on the mantel of performing African American songs as Julie could not. Julie retreats, and Magnolia emerges.

Armed with her own strength and Julie's, at auditions Magnolia "threw back her head then as Jo had taught her, half closed her eyes, tapped time with the right foot, imitative in this, she managed, too, to get into her voice that soft husky Negro quality which for years she had heard on river boats" (275). Ferber represents her skill as entirely derivative; she reaches back for Jo and Queenie's influence in order to achieve marketability. Her performance appears so authentic that the man for whom she is auditioning asks her, "'You a nigger?'" in a replay of Julie's showboat disaster. Although she responds, significantly stumbling over the word, "'No, I'm not a—nigger,'" he says, "'No offense. I've seen 'em lighter'n you'" (275–76). The exchange also harks back to Fenger's asking Fanny if she is Jewish in *Fanny Herself*. Fanny attempts to pass, and then excoriates herself for it; Magnolia tells the truth about her background, but employs the implications of the pass for her own benefit. As in *Fanny Herself*, the interchange accentuates the very real connotations of a life lived behind a mask, in which Magnolia's declaration cements her security. The man asks that she return once she knows some "'real coon songs'" (276) and, reversing her position from the bachelor party, Magnolia resolves to learn the commercially popular songs, teaching herself one called "Whose Black Baby Are You?" She leaves authenticity behind and panders to her audience, but in doing so, redeems herself. With this skill, Magnolia earns the money to keep Kim in convent school even after Gay leaves for good. Her ability to don an African American persona while she herself is palatably white on the stage translates into self-sufficiency.

Magnolia's consumer-friendly songs serve her well, and by appropriating the culture of Jo and Queenie, her vaudeville career ensures a life without economic hardship. Kim becomes an actress over her mother's protests, echoing Selina's when Dirk opts for the practical route of finance over the artistically fulfilling architecture, and the novel flashes forward to Kim's dressing room, where she is waited on by a "mulatto girl in black silk so crisp, and white batiste cap and apron so correct that she might have doubled as stage and practical maid" (282). This seemingly superfluous description nevertheless evokes the theme of elision between performance and reality. Magnolia's life always seems to exist simultaneously onstage and off. Race in America, Ferber's novel suggests, is artifice as much as reality. The maid's appearance underscores the instability of racial designation, recalled by the black and white fabrics that evoke Magnolia and Julie's farewell embrace. Ultimately, Magnolia leaves Kim in New York and heads back to the *Cotton Blossom*, left to her in Parthy's will. Aboard, she finds the racist Elly, who remembers Magnolia as "darkcomplected" (287), eliding Julie and Magnolia's identities in the retelling of the show boat's history. Returned to this context, Magnolia thrives: "She had never left it . . . they were real. The others were dream people" (286). For Magnolia, the stage is "realer" than anyone she encounters in her life with Gay or her daughter. Berlant argues that "*Show Boat* is a strongly ambivalent text, whose critical historicism addresses racial violence, sexual suffering, and class exploitation as problems over which the right kind of narrative might stage a victory of sorts: like making someone laugh or forget to cry so that you can have the power and pleasure of their consolation" (2008, 71). The motives embedded in *Show Boat* push this idea farther since this victory constitutes the very goal of both stage and fiction. The ideas that rendered *Show Boat* a timeless enough story to form a "supertext" exist foremost in the novel.

The year *Show Boat* was published, Ferber inserted herself into a controversy over the fence at the Central Park reservoir, which had been erected to prevent suicides. She didn't like the way it looked, and she tried to gather other New Yorkers to her side in a letter the *New York Times* titled, "The Fenced-In Reservoir": "Won't you please take a look at the atrocity yourself and help me tear it down? Because if you don't I will scramble over the thing myself some dark night in spite of its height and you will see me floating on the first page next morning, face up—just to spite them" (1926, 24). With this mordant, tongue-in-cheek threat, she proclaimed in the same letter that she was not "a marcher in parades nor a signer of protests" (24). Perhaps not. But she put forth her views in her fiction in as forceful a way as she did in such tart editorial letters. Her argument was less defined, more questioning, as she navigated the Mississippi River. An ever-changing stage atop a constantly moving river provided the perfect theater for her ruminations and portrait of a troubled racial and societal American scene. In *Show Boat,* race is performed as well as innate; cultural borrowing and appropriation lead to survival; and mixture reveals its potential societal hazards as well as its strength. The primacy of narrative motivates *Show Boat*'s characters to fight for the right to tell and perform their own stories, seen as a life-giving imperative as well as an artistic goal. With its complex and often problematic discussion of racial topics demonstrating the damage racial hegemony can wreak, *Show Boat* itself becomes rapacious, like the ravenous Mississippi upon which it travels, "a tawny tiger, roused . . . burying its fangs deep in the shore to swallow at a gulp land, houses, trees, cattle—humans, even" (1926, 3).

4

THE COWBOYS, THE INDIANS, AND THE JEW
Cimarron

NOT LONG BEFORE SHE DIED IN 1968, Ferber considered writing a book about American Indians.[1] She visited schools and families in tribal communities from Florida to Arizona, taking her usual, copious notes on her experiences. She considered different protagonists: a young anthropologist, a historian, and a worker on the reservation. But Ferber never resolved the lead-character question because she never wrote the novel, leaving forever open the question of what she would have done with a chance to rewrite her original rumination centered on American Indians: the 1929 Oklahoma epic *Cimarron*, a novel that reaped tremendous financial success, but troubled Ferber both at the time of its publication and as she watched her legacy take shape. "All the critics and the hundreds of thousands of readers took *Cimarron* as a colorful romantic Western American novel," she wrote in *A Peculiar Treasure*, even though to her, the novel was "a malevolent picture" (1939, 302). She meant to do more with *Cimarron* than excite audiences with a cowboy-and-Indians story, and with its focus on racial tension, appropriation, and the construction of society, she did.

1. There is, of course, a long-standing debate over what people such as the Osage tribe or nation featured in *Cimarron* should be called. Ferber used "Indians," and for a time, it seemed that "Native Americans" would be the more appropriate term. Although most tribes prefer to be called by their tribal name—Nez Perce, Osage, Cherokee—recently, "American Indian" has regained currency, and I will use that.

Cimarron uses the founding of the new state of Oklahoma to throw into relief the anxieties surrounding nation-building, particularly when the colonization of another nation—in this case, the Osage—is already in place. Through investigation of the intersections of ethnic and racial tensions inherent within the formative process, Ferber tells the story of the Oklahoma Sooners and how a territory became its own peculiar state.

While researching Cimarron, Ferber corresponded with a man named Fred E. Sutton, who wrote: "You ask if I can give you any information about some of the more important marriages of the Osages with white people" (Letter [1929], 1). Ferber's usual themes may have been on her mind as she planned her Oklahoma novel, but she faced unusual adversity. In the Tulsa Tribune, a local reviewer named Hilda Downing claimed to approve of Cimarron, but also hinted at the trouble Ferber experienced as she interviewed Oklahomans. "There are those who distort Miss Ferber's brusqueness and charming frankness into snobbishness," she wrote (3). She may have been referring to a anti-Semitic depiction of Ferber in a Bartlesville, Oklahoma, newspaper: "'Say, Big Boy,' [Ferber] blatted in that tone children of the Ghetto are apt to use after about the third shot of Oklahoma corn, 'I know my business'" (Gilbert 1978, 361). As Heidi Kanaga writes, "Her putative racial allegiances as a Jewish American were viewed as incongruent and in fact inimical to the appropriate origin of the 'authentic' Western chronicle" (2003, 184). Locals (as presaged by the "Say, Big Boy" quotation) were unappeased, and continued to disparage the novel until Cimarron became a movie starring Irene Dunne and Richard Dix in 1931, and won the Academy Award for Best Picture. Ferber called it "the finest motion picture that has ever been made of any book of mine" (A Peculiar Treasure [1939], 303). Once Oklahoma was placed onscreen, residents were happy to see the story in what they considered a more favorable and glamorous light. (Some consider Cimarron to have another, different iteration other than the film, as Ann Shapiro writes in her article "Edna Ferber: Jewish American Feminist": "There is no doubt that Richard Rodgers and Oscar Hammerstein read Cimarron and were influenced by the work of their friend and colleague, Edna Ferber, when they wrote their hit musical [Oklahoma!]" (2002, 55–56).

The novel itself never gained the affection reserved for either film or any version of the musical, although non-Oklahoma reviewers acknowl-

edged that it did contain the Ferber stamp of sweeping historical portrayal. "Cimarron is not the sort of book one reads again and again for
beauties newly discovered," said the *New York Times Book Review* article,
"Miss Ferber's Vivid Tale": "it is a book which one reads once with avidity,
for a picture that remains indelible" (1930, 3). That picture fits in with
the indelible society Ferber portrays in the novel, in which the early years
of the Oklahoma territory affect a widely varied cast of characters who
live in the town of Osage, a land-rush town named after the local tribe.
Cimarron deals with the ethnic and racial anxieties—white settlement,
relations between African Americans and the Osages, a wandering Jewish
peddler seeking a home—that arise as the territory defines itself. These
tensions and blends form an overlapping pattern of discrimination and
empathy that become an America writ small, where settlement gives rise
both to emotional and literal bloodshed as well as a productive future,
undertaken by turns reluctantly and auspiciously.

Yancey Cravat, a larger-than-life newspaperman, is the outsized character at the heart of *Cimarron*. A talented raconteur, the most accomplished gunslinger in town, an avowed friend (and mysteriously possible
relation) of the Osage people, he is a local legend, nicknamed "Cimarron." Yancey cultivates a picturesque appearance: "His black locks he
wore overlong, so that they curled a little about his neck in the manner of
[the actor Edwin] Booth. . . . [H]is feet were small and arched like a woman's" (1929, 9). Like Gaylord Ravenal's, Yancey's dandyish looks imbue
him with the appearance of a performer. From his questionable gender—
"like a woman's"—to his identification with the American Indian's race
and culture, Yancey offers a heterogeneous, complex identity, a fitting
symbol of the troubled and emergent West that Ferber depicted.

Ferber also codes Yancey's wife, Sabra Cravat, in a multifaceted way.
She forms a foil to his dynamic, heedless character. She comes from a
southern family, migrated to Kansas, but is nevertheless steeped in old
local customs. Sabra represents a robust amalgamation of widely varied
ethnic and regional types: "There was in her the wiry endurance of the
French Marcy; the pride of the Southern Venables" (230), Ferber writes.
She was "of the olive-skinned type. . . . [T]here was something more
New England than Southern in the directness of her glance" (7). Sabra's
hybrid and multiple racial and regional identity—a southerner with a

Yankee gaze, an American with French ancestry—grants her strength, from pride to "wiry endurance." This mixture sometimes incites a "Puritan revulsion" (a confounding antipathy, set as it is against her New England "glance") "against her plumes, her silks, her faintly Latin beauty" (95). Sabra's "Latin" appeal along with her luxurious style of dress renders her foreign to the hardscrabble Anglo Oklahomans of Osage, even to the point of "revulsion." Even with her olive skin, Sabra's "blue-bloodedness" remains paramount. Instead of marrying the questionably raced Yancey, Ferber writes, Sabra's "cerulean stream might have mingled with the more vulgarly sanguine life fluid of any youth in Wichita" (12). The hematological imagery evokes the mixture of Yancey's potentially American Indian blood with Sabra's Anglophonic blood, an American flag's color scheme's worth of ethnic symbology.

Yancey and Sabra's differences of opinion concerning American Indians provide much of the novel's force, and echo Ferber's contradictory descriptions of the Osage nation throughout the novel. Yancey uses seemingly boundless energy to help the Osage while Sabra's determination to forge a life for her family in Osage is matched only by her desire to keep them from the Osage people, a predictably disappointing plan. Early in *Cimarron*, a sage friend advises Sabra as she readies for her trip from Kansas to Oklahoma: "'There's no such thing as a new country for the people who come to it. They bring along their own ways and their own bits of things and make it like the old as fast as they can'" (49). This programmed stasis aptly describes Sabra's family, the Venables. Although relocated from Mississippi, they retain the vestiges of antebellum landed gentry, and their "charming ways, remotely Oriental, that were of the South whence they had sprung" (2). Ferber employs the adjective "Oriental" here not to denote Jewishness as she does in *Fanny Herself*, but to describe another brand of "nobility" based upon the venerable Venables' aristocratic southern past. Yet the choice of adjective recalls Sabra's "olive-skinned," and "French" appearance, lending her some of Fanny's "oriental" gravitas in *Fanny Herself*.

Obligation to tradition dictates that a young African American servant boy fans the family as they dine, even though "Wichita had first beheld this phenomenon aghast; and even now, after twenty years, it was a subject for local tongue waggings" (1929, 6). The Venables' Afri-

can American servants may shock their more egalitarian neighbors, but
the imprint of the South remains strong at the bleeding Kansas dinner
table, rendering the newest of frontiers as feudal as the Confederate-era
South itself. Despite their having relocated, the family derides Yancey
for his desire to settle in new territory, scoffing that the presence of "savages" will keep the territory from achieving statehood. Yancey pushes his
father-in-law, asking:

> "Would you call Chief Apushmataha a savage?"
>
> "Certainly, sir! Most assuredly."
>
> "How about Sequoyah? John Ross? Stand Watie? Quanah Parker?
> They were wise men. Great men."
>
> "Savages, with enough white blood in them to make them leader
> of their dull-witted, full-blooded brothers. The Creeks, sir" (he pro-
> nounced it "suh") intermarried with niggers. And so did the Choc-
> taws; and the Seminoles down in Florida."
>
> Yancey smiled his winning smile. "I understand while you South-
> erners didn't exactly marry—." (41)

Even Yancey's allusion to miscegenation fails to make Venable realize the
ludicrousness of his criticism of race mixing between American Indians
and white people. Curiously, however, Yancey selects only partially white
American Indian leaders to illustrate his point: Chief Apushmataha (c.
1760–1824) was a Choctaw chief, Sequoyah (1767–1843) was a Cherokee
who created a Cherokee syllabary, John Ross (1790–1866) was a Cherokee chief who was seven-eights Scottish, Stand Watie (1806–1871) was
a Confederate general, and Quanah Parker (c. 1840–1911) was the last
chief of the Quahadi Comanche tribe. Thus, he is vulnerable to Venable's
attack. Venable points to intermarriage with African Americans as the
most repugnant characteristic in the tribes he mentions, while Yancey's
shining examples are also products of intermarriage, albeit with white
people. Mixture, so repellent to Venable, has given Yancey his idols. In
fact, Yancey's view is almost as chauvinistic as his father-in-law's, since he
portrays American Indian heritage as an ingredient for a recipe that will
result in sterling leaders. The Osage tribe has a different tradition from
the Seminole and Choctaw whom Venable mentions, since, as Ferber

writes, "The Osage alone had never intermarried with the negro. Except for intermingled white blood, the tribe was pure" (142). "Purity" can apparently sustain even with the addition of white blood, keeping Yancey's syllogism intact. By Venable's lights, race mixture is only objectionable when it includes African Americans.

Yancey may have another, more personal, reason to admire these leaders. The question of his racial identity, based upon his frequent visits to local tribes and ability to duplicate a death cry, provides fuel for local gossips who construct his legend, and "say he has Indian blood in him. They say he has an Indian wife somewhere, and a lot of papooses" (11). Yancey replies enigmatically to these reports of his mixed blood. Although his identity is never spelled out, American Indian ancestry is alluded to, with his shadow-casting hair a sort of inheritor of the "pinprick" of African American blood that dooms Julie in *Show Boat*. Yancey sympathizes with minorities, including Isaiah, the African American servant with the fan, who stows away with the Cravats, and becomes the vector for the complexity of translating regional custom and bigotry in Oklahoma. Sabra takes her father's anti-Indian stance, which Yancey automatically refers back to a slavery framework. "'How about these stories you've told me all your life about the love you Southerners had for your servants and how old Angie was like a second mother to you?' 'Niggers are different. They know their place'" (294). Yancey is armed against any defense of slavery, and the change of scene to an untapped frontier provides him with the stage he needs. The virtue of class humility has little meaning in the new West, something that Yancey comprehends far better than Sabra.

Sabra's racism takes a paternalistic tone. She believes that "[t]he little black boy Isaiah was as much her slave as though the Emancipation Proclamation had never been" (64). Ferber's diction seems to take a step backward in *Cimarron*, where African American imagery deviates from the very human differences encoded in *Show Boat* characters such as Julie and Jo, Queenie and Mose. Isaiah is continually likened to an animal. He sleeps "anywhere, like a little dog" (57), and, frightened, creeps "'between [Yancey's] legs like a whimpering little dog'" (37). Isaiah clearly understands his own marginalized place in both Kansas and Oklahoma, for when he becomes the caregiver to the Cravat children, he tells them traditional stories of "the sorrows and tribulations of a wronged people and their inevitable reward in the after life" (58). Without directly confronting the inequity of his situation, Isaiah uses literary and narrative frameworks to call attention to his background.

Sabra's attitude cannot protect "her slave" entirely, and the local white cowboys torture Isaiah, forcing him to "dance" by shooting at his feet (111). The entire legacy of slavery—master and slave—conveys from the South to Oklahoma. In fact, Yancey's first editorial as editor of the Osage newspaper is titled: "'Shall the Blue Blood of the Decayed South Poison the Red Blood of the Great Middle West?'" (12). His fear is a step backward. For Yancey, there are two distinct races of Americans in Oklahoma, one a pollutant and one pure, one moribund and one vigorous. The South is "poison" to the vigor of the territories. Southern indolence also merges with female commerce in Dixie Lee, Osage's town prostitute, "a descendant of decayed Southern aristocracy" (145).

Yancey wants to see Oklahoma as something new, a place where old societies such as the antebellum South hold no sway. Yet in her own way, and despite her origins, Dixie Lee forces southernness into the future because she is a "shrewd saleswoman," and "harlotry, heretofore a sordid enough slut in a wrapper and curling pins, came to Osage in silks and plumed, with a brain behind it and a promise of prosperity in its gaudy train" (146). With her over-the-top regionally identified name, a nickname for the South coupled with the hero of the Confederacy, evoking the "decayed" world she comes from, Dixie Lee, like the prostitutes with whom Magnolia socializes in *Show Boat,* nevertheless uses her intelligence and capability to promote her own business. Like the backward-thinking Venables, her aristocratic forbears may be derelict and suspect, but Dixie Lee herself embodies a brash brand of western pioneer.

Isaiah, another inheritor of southern traditions, throws the novel's tension into high relief in a moment of carnival when he dresses in Yancey's cast-off clothes, mimicking Yancey's walk to become a "complete picture of Yancey Cravat in ludicrous—in grotesque miniature" (136). These costumed moments recall the burlesque world of *Show Boat,* and serve to underscore the artifice endemic in the new world to which Isaiah has come. Such scenes would become focal points for Ferber's novels—they occur again in *Saratoga Trunk* and *American Beauty*—and as with Isaiah's performance, they expose the latent transgressions and conflicts at the novels' cores. With this scene, the novel's voice seems to stammer, caught between "ludicrous" and "grotesque," as if between Yancey and Sabra's opinions. Sabra angers, believing the boy is mocking her husband, but Yancey views the situation differently: "The black face gazed up at him. In it was worship, utter devotion. Yancey, himself a born actor, knew that in Isaiah's grotesque costume, in his struttings and swaggerings, there had been only that sincerest of flattery, imitation of that which was adored. The eyes were those of a dog, faithful, hurt, bewildered. . . . [He] let his fine white hand rest a moment on the woolly poll" (137).

Yancey bases his understanding of Isaiah's impersonation as loving upon empathy. The passage emphasizes that Yancey, too, is an actor, although his motives remain deliberately opaque. Either he is performing as an Indian with his war cry and understanding of tribal ways, or passing as a non-Indian to Sabra. Yancey's crowds applaud rather than jeer, and he keeps them wondering who is on stage alongside him, and who forms his audience. Yet Isaiah's performance forces Sabra's hand. Her sharpness exposes the deep-seated fears, reinforced by the novel's secrecy about his background, that Yancey is not all he seems, and that Oklahoma society will dramatically remold and alter her entrenched understanding of the world's hierarchies and her own superiority within. Questions of race remain at the forefront as the personality of the charismatic—but borderline bizarre—Yancey unfolds.

The novel itself reflects the ambivalence embodied by its characters, as in the descriptions of the local tribe and the nearby villagers. Some "half-breed children," Ferber writes, were "like a litter of puppies tumbling about a bitch " (120). Yet she also writes that "[t]he Osages, unlike many of the other Territory Plains tribes, were a handsome people—tall, broad shouldered, proud. . . . The town treated them with less consideration than the mongrel curs that sunned themselves in the road" (165). Except that both of Ferber's descriptions of the Osage people employ canine imagery, they have little in common. One describes an animal-like group of people, while the other chastises the "town" (read: white settlers) that treats the Osages like mongrels, dogs whose primary feature is their lack of breeding as they loll in the street.

Yancey endures no such ambivalence. He writes multiple editorials outlining the plight of the Osage nation, all summed up in his epithet

"Let the Red Man live a free man as the White man lives" (281). When Sabra insists that their son learn about "something besides those dirty thieving Indians," she offers instead "George Washington and Jefferson Davis and Captain John Smith," a list which only prompts Yancey to ask if the Smith she means is "the one who married Pocohantas" (61). That comment, in turn, emphasizes the novel's preoccupation with intermarriage, and, in fact, a cousin warns Sabra of having "a Pocohantas for a daughter-in-law" (193), preying on the fear of miscegenation that haunts any practiced bigot.[2]

Where Ferber herself stands on such issues remains questionable. The animalistic descriptions of the "litter" of half-Indian children notwithstanding, in *A Peculiar Treasure*, Ferber sides firmly with Yancey: "It was then that I heard the story of the American Southern Indians driven forth into exile by the American government—as fine an example of minority persecution and injustice as any historian would care to see" (1939, 291). Yet at times throughout *Cimarron*, Ferber's authorial voice counters Yancey's pro-Osage rhetoric: "Yet the plight of the Indian was not as pitiable as Yancey painted it. He cast over them the glamour of his own romantic nature. The truth was that they themselves cared little—except a few of their tribal leaders, more intelligent than the rest. They hunted a little, fished, slept, visited from tribe to tribe. . . . The men were great poker players, having learned the game from the white man, and spent hours at it" (1929, 281).

Except the nod about the poker games, which could be blamed on white settlers' influence, this passage rings with anti-American Indian sentiment, casting the "red men" Yancey defends as largely lazy, apathetic, and unintelligent. Yet their indolence is not self-driven, but "learned from the white man" in the form of the endless poker games. The thrust of how the Indians have grown apathetic—why they "cared little"—has to do with the current predicament of the Osage people under attack. Less ambiguous is Sabra, who levels a vitriolic summary of her Osage neighbors at Yancey: "You and your miserable dirty Indians! You're always going on about them as if they mattered! The sooner they're all dead the better"

2. Of course, Pocahontas actually married an Englishman named John Rolfe, not John Smith.

(117). Sabra's unbridled bigotry might be linked to her husband's preferring the company of the Osage to his family, but its viciousness exposes
the depth of her antipathy toward the very people whose land she now
inhabits and aims to "civilize" to her own satisfaction.

Redoubling and problematizing the cast of ethnic others in Osage is
a man named Sol Levy, or, as most of the people in town call him, "the
Jew" (180). Like Ford in *The Girls*, Sol is one of the overlooked Jewish
characters in the Ferber canon. As solidly as Ferber leans on stereotypes
to describe Isaiah, and despite her own Jewish background and history of
writing more nuanced Jewish characters such as Clarence and Fanny in
Fanny Herself, she relies upon similarly hackneyed phrases to depict her
Jewish character. Levy begins the book as weak, bookish, and easily victimized, much like Clarence before he subverts stereotype and becomes
an adventurer and nature writer. Sol Levy is granted fewer Heyl or Fanny-
like choices—he lacks even *The Girls'* Ford's courage and brilliance—but
initially fulfills instead some of the oldest, tiredest characteristics in the
anti-Semitic glossary.

A peddler, Levy is "bent almost double, gnomelike and grotesque,
against the western sky" (1929, 180), as he hawks his wares. The images of overwork and inhuman physicality seem to have followed him
from "the noisome bowels of some dreadful ship" that brought him to
America. "His hair was blue-black and very thick and his face was white
in spite of the burning Southwest sun. . . . [H]e had the faintly Oriental
look sometimes seen in the student type of his race," Ferber writes (181).
Some of Sol's physicality matches Sabra's, of the "Oriental" Venables, but
more deliberately fuses with the brand of orientalism employed in *Fanny
Herself*, which includes scholarly acumen. In the Wild West of *Cimarron*,
however, this intelligent nobility has obvious drawbacks, since it sets him
against physically skilled white men like Yancey, whose capabilities as
marksmen and equestrians are more crucial to survival than their intelligence. Sol is "a little afraid" of his horse, since he "came from a race of
scholars and traders" (182). Sol possesses none of the physical stamina
necessary to succeed as a rancher or cowboy in a new western town such
as Osage, and embodies the stereotype of Jews as physically weak, but intellectually strong.

The Osage residents employ the same saws Ferber consults. The town prostitutes tease Sol, saying, "'Jews is all rich'" (183), but Sol never employs them. Instead, Sol and the madam Dixie Lee form their own platonic friendship, since both are "outcasts . . . he because of his race, she because of her calling" (183). The association of Jewishness and trade mingles with Dixie Lee's version of commerce until prostitute and Jewish merchant form an allegiance of "outcasts" who prove necessary to the town, but are simultaneously made unwelcome. Although Dixie Lee and Sol both sell things people want, they remain at arm's length from the larger community.

Sometimes difference invites hostility as well, and the unlettered Osage cowboys shoot at Sol as they do at Isaiah (this brutal game seems the most popular pastime in Osage) since "[h]e was a person apart. . . . They looked upon him as fair game" (184). Unlike Isaiah, however, Sol is allowed his own documented opinion of his tormentors: "He thought of them as savages," Ferber writes (184). As they attack, Sol backs into a roadside feed scale:

> He had no weapon. He would not known how to use it if he had possessed one. He was not of a race of fighters. . . . His head lolled a little on one side. His thick black locks hung dank on his forehead At that first instant of seeing him as he rushed out of his office, Yancey thought, subconsciously, "He looks like—like—." . . . It was only later that he realized of Whom it was that the Jew had reminded him as he stood there, crucified against the scale. (184–85)

Through Ferber's unquiet imagery, in his meekness and lack of self-defense, Sol becomes Jesus, just as Selina in *So Big* morphs into Mary as she lies in her wagon at the farmer's market. Reversing the long-held image of Jews as Christ-killers, a Jew is "crucified" for his Jewishness. Yancey rescues Sol, telling him that Oklahoma does not suit him because he comes from "'a race of dreamers'" (186), as if Sol's vagueness rather than his ethnicity forced his victimization. Sol is able to rally his best noble oriental-Jewish retort, a version of that used by Fanny and Ford to turn away negative comments about being Jewish: "'Those barbarians!

My ancestors were studying the Talmud and writing the laws the civilized world now lives by when theirs were swinging tree to tree'" (187). Once again, the venerable age of Jewishness serves to prove its culture and importance, even as its focus renders Sol a bit of a passive victim rather than a valiant rescuer like Yancey.

Despite the personal commitment implicit in his dramatic rescue efforts, Yancey vanishes from Osage for years at a time, while Isaiah comes of age and falls in love with Arita Red Feather, an Osage woman who also works for the Cravats, and whose hybridized way of speaking foretells Ferber's vision of a blended Oklahoma: Arita's "native Osage, Sabra's refined diction, and Isaiah's Southern negro accent were rolled into an almost unintelligible jargon" (211). The pairing ends disastrously when Arita bears Isaiah's baby. The Osage people brutally kill all three: Arita and the baby left to roast in the sun in a fastened, untanned hide, and Isaiah murdered with a rattlesnake. Anticipating the reader's horror at these gruesome murders, Ferber notes in *Cimarron*'s foreword that "the death of Isaiah" is "based on actual happenings" (ix). Even Ferber at her most dramatic, she seems to say, could not dream up something so horrific.

"[T]he thing that had happened to the black boy was so dreadful, so remorseless that when the truth of it came to Sabra she felt all this little world of propriety, of middle class Middle West convention that she had built up about her turning to ashes under the sudden flaring fire of hidden savagery. . . . Her hatred of the Indians now amounted to an obsession" (239). With the family's murder, Sabra is now identified not only with the South and then with Puritan ideals, but also now with the Midwest and its "convention," as if a less bourgeois person could have comprehended the terrifying crimes. The sinister image of "hidden savagery" demonstrates Sabra's state of mind toward her Osage neighbors, but also implies that a portion of Oklahoma is secreted from and untamable to its newcomers. While his murder increases Sabra's antipathy toward the Osages, it also allows her to realize some of her own shortcomings, reversing her patronizing attitude toward Isaiah, if tragically too late: "Isaiah had been a faithful black child in her mind, whereas he was, in reality, a man grown" (241).

Sabra and Yancey's son, Cimarron Cravat, fulfills the other side of the intermarriage portent delivered by the Venables in marrying Ruby Big

Elk, the daughter of an Osage chief, a union that delights Yancey, who sees it as the perfect model for Oklahoma's future, and horrifies Sabra. Ferber describes the chief in theatrically laden language: "His long locks, hanging about his shoulders, straight and stiff, were dyed a brilliant orange, like an old burlesque queen's" (353). Like Yancey, Chief Big Elk's appearance is feminized through an aspect of performance, although unlike Yancey, who resembles an actor, Chief Big Elk's hair is colluded with a stagey, out-of-date femininity, suggesting that what succeeds as panache in Yancey is ludicrous in Big Elk. For Sabra, the effects of the new alliance revert to ethnic description. With the shock of the new in-laws, "It was at times like this that the Marcy in her stood her in good stead. She came of iron stock, fit to stand the fire" (355). Sabra's latent fear of hybrid descendants is ironic, considering her own heterogeneous identity, with her ability to handle a shock like intermarriage a result of her "iron stock." Sabra imagines the Osages' eyes as "dead," like Julie's eyes in *Show Boat,* and considers the news "monstrous" (355), alluding to her belief that the Osage people are somehow less human than she, and that her son is on the verge of an unearthly union. "One grotesquerie proved too much for her strained nerves and broke them. . . . Sabra thought, I am dying, I am dying" (357). Communion with the Osage people and their otherworldly and "grotesque" customs terrifies her nearly to death, pushing her closer to her antagonists with their own "dead" features.

Yancey thrills to this fulfilling and hybrid wedding, the goal of his own preoccupation with varied ways of life and people. In fact, he sees the union as a symbol of his ideology. "'This is Oklahoma,'" he tells Sabra. "'In a way it's what I wanted it to be when I came here twenty years ago. Cim's like your father, Lewis Venable. Weak stuff, but good stock. Ruby's pure Indian blood and a magnificent animal. It's hard on you now, my darling. But their children and their grandchildren are going to be such stuff as Americans are made of'" (357). Donna Campbell writes that "Cim Cravat's matter-of-fact adoption of Osage ways demonstrates that cultural reciprocity and pride in identity, not assimilation, is the fulfillment of Yancey's dream" (2003, 35). But Yancey's dream stretches even further than Campbell notes, further into the future even than the long-reaching book details. His definition of "Americans" includes his descendants, who will embody the swirling recipe of ethnicity he lists. Perhaps he does not

desire assimilation, as Campbell suggests, in the sense of one culture becoming subsumed into another. He does, however, seek a blend of Ruby
and Cim's "blood," and even employs a name for these perfectly blended
people: Americans.

Cim and Ruby's wedding brings into focus some of the more outlying
members of Oklahoma society, as well. The newly oil-rich couple's hired
girl is white, with "hair so light a yellow as to appear almost white. Her
unintelligent eyes were palest blue. Her skin was so fair as to be quite
colorless. In the midst of the roomful of dark Indian faces the white face
of the new Cravat hired girl seemed to swim in a hazy blob" (1929, 358).
With their money, the Osage people have achieved a reversal of fortune,
where they have made servants of the very people who, like Sabra, view
them as grotesque inferiors. Ferber's description of the servant's extreme
whiteness, with her transparent eyes and "colorless" skin, demonstrates
a "hazy blob" of an identity ready to be absorbed into the next generation,
unable to keep itself separate. Such ghostlike pallor can never prevail in a
future that will see what "Americans are made of," as Yancey says. Money,
more than whichever "stock" is strongest, determines the American ruling class. The Osage people have risen to the top because of their financial shift, embodying the American ability of money, as in *The Girls*, to
turn firefighters into operagoers, or colonizers into servants.

The victory of the oil money—white servants, luxury, entitlement—
exacts its toll, however. The Oklahoma society Ferber frames through
Yancey turns itself upside down: "The Osage Indian men were broad
shouldered, magnificent, the women tall, stately. Now they grew huge
with sloth and overfeeding" (1929, 344–5). Even though they are moneyed, however, the same complaints exist about the Osage that were aired
when the tribe was locked in poverty. Ferber describes an Osage account
book during the oil boom: "The white man's eye, traveling down the tidy
list, with its story-book Indian names . . . rejected what it read as being
too absurd for the mind to grasp. Clint Tall Meat $523,000" (340). That
a wealthy member of the Osage tribe is "absurd" when he achieves the
trappings of wealth demonstrates why intermarriage is so radical: if the
"white man's eye" cannot even comprehend that someone named Clint
Tall Meat can be rich, then mixed-race children—and a future in which
all Americans are descendants of more than one people—are even more

incomprehensible, and yet inevitable through such pioneers as Cim and Ruby, even at the cost of Isaiah and Arita, and with the specter of their grisly end.

In these fat times, another ethnic "other" finds prosperity. Sol makes a success of his store by changing along with the town of Osage as it metamorphoses from a rough western town to an oil-rich and sophisticated village. He lives up to the idea of a Jew as outlandish by maintaining a zoo at his store, making him the owner of a kind of a Wall Drug of the 1880s. Yet Sol struggles in spite of his financial ease: "Although Sol Levy was still the town Jew, respected, prosperous, the town had never quite absorbed this Oriental. A citizen of years' standing, he still was a stranger" (284). Sol's "Orientalism" in this case accounts for his distance, as he stands socially—and intellectually—away from the people with whom he trades every day. At town social events,

> Sol remained aloof. He regarded the hot, sweaty, shouting dancers with a kind of interested bewilderment and wonder, much as the dancers themselves sometimes watched the Indians during one of the Festival Dances on the outlying reservations. On occasion he made himself politely agreeable to a stout matron well past middle age. They looked up at his tragic dark eyes; they noticed his slim ivory hand as it passed them a plate of cake or a cup of coffee. "He's real nice when you get to know him," they said. "For a Jew, that is." (284)

Here Sol allies himself with spectators, with himself observing the white citizens of the town at the recreative social activity in the same way those people viewed the Osage dancers, leaving him on top or to the side in a hierarchy that saves him from being observed. Sol's "dark" eyes and "ivory hand" are similar to Julie's in *Show Boat*, demonstrating his apartness even in terms of color, and the ways in which his ethnicity, too, represents mystery, and something to be hidden. The inborn Jewish suffering that Clarence explains to Fanny in *Fanny Herself* lies inherent in Sol's "tragic" eyes, and his earlier association with Jesus erodes in place of a new one in which he emerges victorious alongside the newly wealthy Osages. Seizing upon this elevation, Yancey decides that Sol should run for the position of mayor of Osage, which galls some of the inhabitants—

"'A Jew for mayor of Osage! They'll be having an Indian mayor next. . . . And as for me, why, I can trace my ancestry right back to William Whipple, who was one of the signers of the Declaration of Independence'" (1929, 285). Of course, the irony is that the Osage people lived in America much longer ago than William Whipple, and Sol points out that his people, in turn, are even older, maintaining Ferber's emphasis on Jews' ancient heritage. He follows the Jew-as-noble-Oriental model and retorts that Yancey should "'[t]ell her one of my ancestors wrote the Ten Commandments. Fella name of Moses'" (285).

The Levy Mercantile Company profits so much that it occupies an entire square block, and with Yancey's continued absences, Sol supports Sabra. Also, with his wealth, Sol

> had built a type of penthouse after his own plans. It was the only one of its kind in all Oklahoma. . . . It was . . . filled with the rarest of carpets, rugs, books, hangings. Super radio, super phonograph, super player piano. Music hungry. There he lived, alone, in luxury, of the town, yet no part of it. At sunset, in the early morning, late of a star-spangled night he might have been seen leaning over the parapet of his sky house, a lonely little figure, lean, ivory, aloof, like a gargoyle brooding over the ridiculous city sprawled below. (373)

Sol's love of music and books demonstrates his position that keeps him an inheritor of the "race of scholars." He remains above the other townsfolk, literally, looking down with his sophisticated trappings, yet very much an American as the "star-spangled" echo of the anthem attests. As a gargoyle, he is still read as bizarre and "lonely," but adds a note of superiority with his aloofness at the "ridiculous" city, as if holding his neighbors in slight contempt makes up for their disassociation. Jewishness in Oklahoma allows for a shift away from Jewish stereotype, but still forbids full inclusion. Sabra's dependence upon Sol, however, suggests his import and centrality to his community.

In this fraught environment, Cim and Ruby's children live up to the high expectations set for the "Americans" Yancey prophesies. Cim's son Yancey—*Cimarron* is another of Ferber's novels with a confusingly repetitive nomenclature—"was a mixture of a dozen types and forbears—Indian,

Spanish, French, Southern, Southwest. With that long narrow face, the dolichocephalic head, people said he looked like the King of Spain . . . others contended that he was his Indian mother over again" (364). Young Yancey also shows Ferber's anxiety concerning descriptions of the very mixed-race people she so often includes in her novels, as the "dozen" forbears all add their own physical characteristics. Observers grasping at straws such as the King of Spain—a personage as remote as Andy Hawks's putative Basque heritage—demonstrate that tension caused by the ethnically unclassifiable. People desire taxonomies and classification. Indeed, a woman tells Yancey that Oklahoma is all "'oil and dirty Indians,'" to which he replies, "'There is quite a lot of oil, but we're not all dirty'" (372). His physical appearance does not immediately invite identification as an American Indian, but Yancey identifies himself that way, performing almost a reverse pass, and presumably shaming the unwitting bigot into recognizing her blunder. Unlike his grandfather, he does not rely on hearsay and whispers, but self-identifies as Indian.

The grandest change wrought by the interracial marriage is Sabra's conversion to acceptance of the Osage people. While her racism abates in her old age, and she becomes a congresswoman from Oklahoma, the American Indians remain not-quite-equals, but protectorates, almost as she perceived Isaiah at the novel's beginning: "[The Indian] was considered legitimate prey, and thousands of prairie buzzards fed on his richness," Ferber writes (378). Marshaling her paternalism, Sabra tries to help, and her colleagues "conceded that this idea of hers, to the effect that the Indian would never develop or express himself until he was as free as the negro, might some day become a reality" (378). Eliding slavery and the treatment of Indians, Sabra places the two peoples together, positioning the Osage nation as awaiting their own emancipation proclamation in order to avoid predatory white Oklahomans. Considering Isaiah's fate, "free as the negro" seems blindly optimistic, but at least gestures toward a future of some measure of egalitarian treatment, and significant growth on Sabra—and Oklahoma's—part.

Nevertheless, some ideologies stay in place. Sabra commissions a statue of Yancey to commemorate Oklahoma: "Behind him, one hand just touching his shoulder for support, stumbled the weary, blanketed figure of an Indian" (381). While the increasingly itinerant Yancey is likely more "weary" than any Osage, Sabra recreates him as maintaining the position of rescuer while the Osage figure remains subservient. She no longer rages about American Indians, but Sabra's attitude toward them continues problematic and unstable. Ann Shapiro writes that with *Cimarron*, "the outsiders, Yancey and Sabra, create a mythological world where Indians and whites are finally united in a new democratic America" (2002, 55). In other words, the hybridized life Yancey lives achieves reality by the novel's end, pointing the way toward a Yancey-defined future for the state and, by extension, the country. Sabra's personal alliance to Yancey, despite his failings as a husband and father, fortifies her view of him as a hero of the new state.

While young Cim and Ruby's marriage constitutes a union prefiguring the future of racial and ethnic blending in a new state and new society, it is unclear that democracy will prevail in the sense that Shapiro puts forth. Instead, the amalgamation of American Indian and white families may create a new future for Oklahoma, but like the South-burdened Kansas Venables, the state will labor under its residents' history. The novel commits to the notion that, even with age, Sabra's racism never fully resolves. Even though she becomes the representative of the people of Oklahoma, her identity as both matriarch and paternalist endures. Simplicity evades the novel, and Ferber's continued pressure upon each aspect of racial tension in the new territory, from Isaiah's horrible murder to the exorbitant oil wealth of the Osage, presages a world that must continue to grapple as it fulfills its patternless potential.

In *Cimarron*, ethnic mixtures produce widely different and sometimes disastrous results, but all demonstrate their intrinsic power and indicate a future that might include the lessening submergence of their vitality and potency, symbolized by the Osage people becoming less physically imposing. Ferber moved forward from *Show Boat's* images of mixture as inviting disaster or being more appropriate on cultural terms, like Magnolia's singing African American songs. With *Cimarron*, Ferber proves the latent and potentially inflammatory nature of ethnic mixing, but also its potential—and necessity—for a country defining itself, territory by territory.

5

COLORING THE BLUE BLOODS
American Beauty and *Come and Get It*

FERBER'S DEPICTION OF THE EFFECTS of ethnic mixture comes under increasingly complicated and directed scrutiny in the 1931 *American Beauty* and the 1934 *Come and Get It*. Set respectively in New England and the woods of Wisconsin, both novels examine the stressors on Anglo-American hegemony that occur when white immigrants, in these cases Polish or Swedish people, add to the striation of American ethnicities. Although Ferber had touched upon these questions in earlier novels, these mid-career works demonstrate her growing investment in the complexities of the American social hierarchy she had already depicted as volatile, self-propagating, and under consistent revision.

Of course, focusing on white immigrants and how they shaped and were shaped by the communities they integrated brought Ferber into intensely familiar and personal territory. Her own father, a Hungarian immigrant, would not have stuck out because of his skin color but because of his ethnic otherness as a Jew, something Ferber internalized and wrote about in *Fanny Herself*'s passing scene. Ferber's own avowed patriotism showed her desire to identify as American; these novels feature characters undergoing a similar process. To return to John Dewey's formulation, the process for Ferber and her characters includes "connecting the hyphens" in order to build a stronger American identity in a world that did not always foster or even tolerate such mixing.

In *American Beauty*, this process of connection takes place in New England, and begins with the book's title. An American Beauty rose is a French cultivar of "hybrid parentage." Originally sold in America in 1888, the American Beauty was the best-selling varietal far into the 1920s. It is the official flower of Washington, D.C., and with its name and vigor, has worked its way into symbolic import as well as horticultural. For Ferber, the titular image works to emphasize the importance of hybridity in culture. To demonstrate the necessity of this kind of strength, Ferber upends and distorts the idea of American royalty—the New England that lays claim to Mayflower families and the origins of American thrift, hard work, and ingenuity.

Rudyard Kipling wrote to publisher Abner Doubleday to praise *American Beauty,* meanwhile revealing some of his own ethnic anxieties, as Ferber noted in *A Peculiar Treasure:* "'[*American Beauty*] has for me a personal interest because we were in New England just as the outside invasion began, and the last of the old mortgaged to death men were dropping off the naked farms. Mercifully, I didn't see the Poles move in. It was Italians in those days'" (1939, 307). Kipling's unease about the shifting culture of New England demonstrates exactly why Ferber employed Connecticut; its valence as a site maximizes its dramatic potential as well as distilling American tensions of old and new ways of life. In the Connecticut of *American Beauty,* anemic and despondent New Englanders find themselves washed away when Polish immigrants purchase their unproductive farms, altering the physical and demographic landscape. Ferber removes the concept of sickliness from urban immigrants living in unhealthy tenements to afflicted Connecticutians on their similarly weak farms who need new blood. With grotesque characters who symbolize the Puritan ways that refuse to die and a sense of repressed carnival throughout, the novel demonstrates that even America's altar of New England can be forced into an American future in which uselessly "thin blood" dies out in favor of that of earthy, fertile peasants.

Unsurprisingly, many New Englanders loathed this image. As Ferber writes of the novel's reception in *A Peculiar Treasure,* "I had not drawn Connecticut as a mass of rose-embowered cottages half hidden by apple orchards, peopled by broad-shouldered John Aldens and pretty Priscillas. Connecticut was hopping roaring mad" (1939, 307). (John Alden and Priscilla Mullins were, of course, two iconic Mayflower passengers who helped to settle Plymouth, Massachusetts.) Also, Ferber identifies a more menacing impulse in the Connecticut criticism: "What right (one newspaper actually demanded) had a Jew to come into New England and write about it!" (306). Ferber knew very well how defensive a society she was taking on in *American Beauty*, and in order to achieve her ends, she unspools particularly dramatic turns.

To achieve her ethnically aware departure from time-honored pilgrim stories, Ferber draws heavily on Nathaniel Hawthorne's New England, a place full of black veils, forbidding characters, and storied houses like her novel's key site, the old Oakes farm. Teresa Goddu writes that "the gothic, by articulating the abject within American culture, threatens to reveal that America's dearest myths are haunted by history" (1997, 14). Ferber used Goddu's "gothic discourse of decay and degeneracy" to articulate her version of Connecticut, laying bare the "rotten at the core" New England from which Selina shrinks in *So Big*.

Yet if New Englanders despised the novel, its critical reception was not much better. In the *New York Times Book Review*, Margaret Wallace wrote, "Lacking plot, as it does, there was need of a centralization upon a single character to give the book force and unity; and this centralization is lacking. 'American Beauty' falls definitely below the level of Edna Ferber's best work" (1931, 7). On the other hand, the novel inspired at least one reviewer to adopt a Ferberesque tone of hyperbole: "No one, as far as we are aware, has taken the trouble to ascertain the date on which Edna Ferber discovered America, or rather that inconsiderable portion thereof lying outside the Chicago city limits, but there are legal holidays far less worthy of celebration," wrote Frederic F. Van de Water in the *Evening Post*. Even the gushing Van de Water, however, acknowledges that the book has "a lack of symmetry and occasional lapses in fact" (1931, 7). (Connecticut Indians used drums for signaling, he writes, not smoke signals, as Ferber mentions.) Ferber also faced distressed readers who insisted, as politician Tom Taggart did of *Show Boat*, that *American Beauty* was too closely based upon fact. Residents of Brookfield, Connecticut, a town Ferber had visited during her research, insisted that she used details from their lives and utilized too closely one specific house in the novel. The *Boston Transcript* printed a photograph of a farmer and a house, both supposedly models for Ferber. She waved off these claims. "The house exists only in my mind," Ferber retorted during a lecture waggishly titled "Can A Writer Have Imagination?" at Yale in 1932. "I wish I could convey in my writing that I am just pretending and that I am just playing" (qtd. in Gilbert 1978, 352).

The controversy indicates how large Ferber's celebrity and relevance had grown by the time of *American Beauty*'s publication. It also indicates that she accurately judged the level of anxiety that her books incited. If her topics were provocative, they were also effective, and probing at truths that some found patent. Ferber, as always, eschewed anything overly subtle or shaded. In fact, *American Beauty* opens with an old New Englander named True Baldwin driving through Connecticut marveling at changed names on mailboxes, exactly as Selina DeJong does when she views the street signs in *So Big*'s Chicago. He notices "Jackoswski where Mapes had been; Franek instead of Pynchon," this last notably the surname of the family at the center of Hawthorne's 1851 novel *The House of the Seven Gables* (1931, 19). When True notices the farm's prosperity, his daughter says "'But that isn't Yankee. That's Polack'" (5). True retorts: "'I'll show you who New England belongs to, by God, if I have to buy up the whole state of Connecticut'" (6). His comment poses the key question: whom does New England—or, for that matter, America—belong to? The people who can "buy it up," or those who stay and tend the land? True understands the strict striations of New England society more than his apparent anti-immigrant determination would indicate. In his youth, he worshipped a girl at church named Jude Oakes, who sat forward while his family was seated "'way back. There's the caste system for you, in America'" (10). True might claim to comprehend inequality in America, but he fails to internalize the similarities between the class divisions he experiences and the ethnic ones he wishes to create. Sitting in the back row has given him no empathy.

Candace—a female architect, a sort of Emma McChesney for Dirk DeJong's set—sees the old Oakes farm and says, participating in the consumerist impulse, "'I don't care how many Polacks own it, True, you've got to buy me that house and let me restore it'" (22). Class and ethnic assumptions permeate the Baldwins' visit, even on an animal level. Spying a setter, they decide that "'that dog—he's no Polish farmer's dog. He's a thoroughbred'" (25). The dog's handsome owner tells them the farm belongs to a man named Olzzak. True calls the owner a "Polack," and in one of Ferber's Dickensian revelations, the patrician-seeming man himself is the "Polack" in question.

The house Candace longs for may have a name invoking natural stability—Oakes—but stands upon a foundation of contorted physicality and evocations of inbreeding. From the tradition of Cimarron Cravat's "dociocephalic" head comes a family with members such as Big Noel, whose seven-foot height was an inheritance, since "every other generation or so there cropped out in the family one member who seemed to have sprung from some prehistoric race, so vast, so out of proportion to his fellow men'" (40). Even the Oakes house itself retains some of this physical extremism: "It was a legend in the neighborhood that these monoliths had been broken into proper size by a phenomenally powerful Negro slave named Esau who had shaped them by dropping a huge boulder upon them, which stone he first balanced on his head. In lieu of a suitable tool of harder metal, great Esau's skull and the black marble pillar of his neck served very well" (42).

This passage indicates the corporeal—and familial—relationship between the house and the slaves who created it. Esau's head is hard enough to balance a boulder, and he uses his own skull and neck as tools. "Great Esau" is part building and part man, and his "phenomenal" power only serves to underscore his inhuman aspect. A reference to "a tidy little army of Negro slaves" (44) adds to the understanding of whose bodies drive and animate the household. Ferber underscores the horror of slavery in early Connecticut and its importance to the legends surrounding the settling of New England when she mentions a "blithe" advertisement selling an "able body'd wench, 16 years old (with sucking child)" (58). Ferber holds the North just as accountable as the South for slavery, demonstrating a pan-American responsibility for the atrocities in the country's heritage. Corporeality emphasizes the fundamental import of enslaved people within the New England farms.

Furthering the association between the house and bodies is a macabre fact: the body of a daughter of the family named Tamar Oakes, who ran away to live with Indians and dies is buried under the hearthstone, producing a palpably gothic space in the house: "Feeling this dining-room slab something in the nature of a skull at the feast, visitors were wont to

experience that prickling of the scalp . . . that comes with sudden panic"
(52). With troubling events such as Tamar's death and in-home interment
as a background, the Connecticut landscape "settled into the rigor of
death" (65). Jude Oakes must hire help since she has run out of the local
crop of "spring-halted hired men, native to the region, withered twigs of
once-fine family trees" (66). In Ferber's vision, the Puritan heritage is not
the strong bloodline to which organizations such as the Daughters of the
Revolution lay claim, but a decrepit inheritance of livestock deformity—
"spring-halt," and "withered twigs" instead of hardy, life-affirming stock.

The arboreal imagery is furthered by the novel's Polish immigrants,
who nourish the land and provide a physical contrast to the sickly New
Englanders with their hale physiques, "far too heady a draught for the di-
gestion of this timorous New England remnant of a dying people" (69).
The gothic overlay of the area's heritage only expands when Ferber invokes the area's history of witch trials: "In an earlier day Puritan Connecticut and Massachusetts would no doubt have put them to death as
evil beings who bewitched the farms and made them bloom by some
black magic" (68) and, indeed, a neighbor warns the Oakeses that their
new Polish hired man, Ondy Olzzak, comes from a people who make
human sacrifices, "and the women folks are fierce as wild beasts" (78).
These allusions to illicit magic demonstrate the paranoia Ferber's New
Englanders inherited from their witch-hunting ancestors, and ultimately
serve to point up the otherworldly and fearsome characters—far more
similar to those hunted during the Salem trials than any Eastern European immigrant—in their own midst.

These inventions are all related to the decaying Oakes tribe. Ferber
describes Jude's cousin Arabella as having the "body of a giantess, the
bones of a behemoth" (83) similar to her progenitor, "Big Noel." Like
Reverend Hooper in Hawthorne's 1836 story "The Minister's Black Veil,"
Bella "liked to prowl the house late at night, a restless, tortured figure,
black garbed" (99). Jude's dwarf brother Jotham Oakes counters her
hugeness, providing another extreme image of a "withered offspring of a
degenerate clan" (79). Jotham—the first dwarf character of a triumvirate
including Cupide in *Saratoga Trunk* and Scotty in *Come and Get It*—has
an intellectual disability, and Jude places his food on the floor, "as though

he were a little dog. . . . Certainly his pink cheeks and his round blue meaningless eyes and his thick shock of white hair gave him the look of a chubby old baby" (74). The black clothing and distorted bodies and minds of the Oakes family point to a precipitous decline, a threat of what can happen if what is venerated as truly "American"—in this case, New England Anglos and their heritage—is allowed to reign unchallenged.

The gothic nature cannot remain behind the stove, however, and is galvanized to a more public—and stageworthy, in a direct line with the preoccupation with performance in *Show Boat*—appearance by a young member of the family, raised away from New England. Temmie Pring (a Ferber double-name; this Temmie is named Tamar for the ancestor buried beneath the hearth) returns to the family homestead. Ondy sits at the table with "a Connecticut cigar in his hand" (1931, 101), a consumer appropriating Connecticut and its products, when Jude walks in: "The midget stood bent double, his legs apart and his head between his legs, his back to the others in the room, and his face in the frame of his legs engaged in making the most fantastic and blood-curdling contortions, upside down. And in the center of the room, poised on one foot, the other leg stretched out behind her, was a young girl in the costume of a storybook Indian maiden. . . . She was posed as though for an audience" (101).

Not only Jot is upside down in this scene, in which he makes himself more of a spectacle; Jude also sees a reversal of the traditional order in the inheritor of the Oakes family dressed as an Indian, harking back to the original Tamar Oakes, who died yearning to be with the Indians. Temmie wears the costume in which she used to sell tonic with her wayward parents—Jude's lost sister and her dissolute husband—hawking medicine in disguise as "descendant of old Waramug, of the Weantinock tribe, of Connecticut" (103). Temmie recreates herself as one of Indians of Connecticut, subverting the Oakes legacy with its white patrician roots. Jude, "terrible to see," forbids her to wear the dress again (103). Even more than Jot and Bella, Jude represents the decay of the once-strong New Englander because she possesses "the iron of her ancestors; but it had corroded with the years, so that now everything she touched was stained with rust," and the portrait of her ancestor "looked sadly down upon the ruin his descendants had wrought" (128, 163). Jude cannot maintain the past glory of her family name. With corrupt familial descendants such as Temmie, and only Ondy to curate the land, artifacts of decomposition haunt both house and family.

Temmie, with her partially spectator status, particularly highlights the dramatic slippage in economic and social state of both family and home. Raised traveling with a sideshow, she serves as a funnel for the upside-down world the Oakes house symbolizes, so that the freaks with whom they traveled "were more real to her than the gaping, pop-eyed people who stared at them outside the tent, or filed foolishly in to stare again for a dime" (110). Given Temmie's background, the unusual Oakes household does not frighten her, which she proves by falling asleep upon the hearth under which her namesake—the first Tamar—is buried. For Temmie, accustomed to performance, audience members are more foreign than giants and dwarves, whether in her parents' sideshow or in her long-lost family.

For Temmie, the Polish hired man Ondy represents the critical spectator, while he remains an outsider to Jude because of his ethnicity. He possesses physical and sexual appeal, with "strong flexible hands" and "muscular legs" (124), and Ferber describes him as he is viewed: "Women's eyes rested on [his mouth] and their own lips curved and opened a little" (127). Ondy's attractiveness suggests a fertility that stands in marked contrast with the dying and increasingly malformed Oakes family, and portends the inevitable intersection between the Polish and Anglo-Americans. When his pregnant wife arrives from Poland with their son Stas, the couple refuses a doctor's care because "'Pole woman is not like American woman'" (146). Once the baby is born, Temmie wraps her in an old Oakes shawl, and Jude rebels, as if she fears contamination from even the material trappings of the family touching a Polish person: "'I'll have no Oakes dresses on an Olszak'" (152), she declares in a premonition of the mixing to come.

The foreshadowing of donning old Oakes clothing comes to further fruition when the ever-performing Tamar puts on the forbidden clothes of the old Tamar in a moment that forces the novel into increasingly gothic territory: "She looked at the portrait behind her. She looked at herself. Tamar Oakes. Which Tamar Oakes? They were the same. They were one" (177). Ferber describes her laugh as "hysterical" (177), and the passage—the haunted house, a ghost possessing the girl who wants to possess the ghost—produces a fresh round of horror. Taken with her image in the dead girl's clothing, Tamar decides to make it available for public consumption. She plans a show that morphs her past life in the sideshow with her current life as an Oakes, and the haunted Oakes past itself. To complete the performance, Temmie adds her relations, the giant and the dwarf, as well. Ondy, as the barker, turns the family into Jude's gravest fear—a commodity hawked by a non-Oakes—and Jude literally has a stroke seeing that Tamar has made the original Tamar into less a venerated ancestor than a spectacle. That no one comes to the "show" only reinforces the eeriness of Tamar's creepy performance.

"The house lived in daily fear of this helpless, half-dead woman," writes Ferber, an allusion to all of Connecticut living in fear of the half-dead as its culture pitches between past and future. "It was grotesque, it was macabre" (195). Ferber's narration grows shrill with this vision of the Oakes house becoming further haunted by Jude in her new "half-dead" form. Ondy (now widowed) and Temmie marry, and for their wedding night, they select the big front room of the house, with disastrous results. Temmie encounters "[a] grotesquely sprawled thing, its wide-open eyes staring with a terrible glare of suspicion and hate . . . a long bony forefinger pointed straight to where the dead eyes stared—pointed as though in dreadful accusation" (223). The sight of a Polish person sleeping in the ancestral Oakes bed—with the underlying assumption of his sleeping with an Oakes and thus tainting the family bloodline—kills the already-spectral Jude. The threat of ethnic blending polluting the besieged house mortally wounds her, and ensures the family's downfall. Like Quasimodo by Esmerelda's grave in Victor Hugo's novel *The Hunchback of Notre Dame*, published one hundred years earlier, Jot freezes to death at his burial site—another Oakes dead of exposure—and is himself interred in a child's coffin, placed beneath the ground as the new Oakes/Olzzak family continues.

The novel's focus may turn away from the eerie Oakes past and toward the future of the family, but the otherworldly pull of the New England ancestors does not relent. The birth of Temmie and Ondy's son Orrange, named for an illustrious Oakes progenitor, turns his mother into an Oakes along the gothic lines of Jude, mutating her body and character:

"It was as though she had willed [Orrange's birth] against the forces of nature. It left her torn and old, with a pinched and haggard face set permanently on that elfin body" (235). Orrange favors his forbear as much as his mother resembles the first Tamar in the family portraits, and Ondy jokes, "'I betcha feller in picture is his papa, not Ondy'" (235), a comment with an incestuous undertone while, although physically impossible, adds to the air of dark secrets kept hidden beneath the hearth. In his own way, Orrange truly is more the son of his namesake than of Ondy, as he inherits Temmie's obsession with the Oakes homestead, and despite his own father's Polishness, Orrange joins with Temmie in keeping the farm a representative site of the Oakes family.

Stasis is impossible; Ferber casts Polishness as nearly as bizarre as the original toxic New England culture of the novel. "Oakes farm was a curious mixture, now, of Poland and New England" (241), she writes, and "curious" here seems to refer to something menacing rather than quaint, as she elaborates in a later description of Polish-inhabited areas: "All seemed prosperous, serene. Yet underlying and permeating everything was a curiously sinister and hidden thing. There was about these alien people a strange opposition of moods. Now tender, merry; suddenly sullen, brutal" (245). This description represents a marked diversion from the productive and sexually appealing Ondy of earlier in the book. The gothic originally seems the provenance of the decaying New England society, but Ferber describes part of Polish American culture in similar terms, especially the idea that something "curiously sinister and hidden" lies beneath a patina of prosperity. As the families merge, they become more like the old Oakes descendants rather than maturing into a healthful mixture of ethnicities, implying that the connection is not entirely fruitful.

Distinctions sharpen rather than melt into each other. "Tamar was increasingly the New Englander; Ondy more markedly the Pole" (267), Ferber writes, and the hostility created by disparity is symbolized by moments such as when Ondy harshly and clumsily scratches the name "Olszak" onto an Oakes family silver cup. The Polish New Englander does not exist in Ferber's formulation, and Temmie, never a mainstay of the community because of her unusual upbringing and origins, finds herself shunned from all sides: "The sparse New England women eyed her with Brahmin disapproval. . . . That Oakes girl—the one that married the Polack" (243). There is evidently no future for a Connecticut Oakes, with Temmie's attempt to keep her legacy alive thwarted by the oppressively thriving Polish community. Even the dead Oakeses struggle: at the grave-yard burying the giant Bella, the gravestones of the old Puritans are ill tended and overgrown, while the Polish "well-kept graves bloomed with floral pieces of wire and colored glass, glittering in the sunlight'" (283). These industrial touches—wire and glass, mimicking the actual floral ar-rangements often seen on graves—seem somehow tacky, but neverthe-less prove that someone alive still cares.

The novel's conclusion, which circles back to Constance and True, sees the Oakes house and farm for sale because Polish-identified fam-ily members want the money rather than the decaying farm. Connecti-cut becomes a contested site in which "[t]he Pole moved to the city, and the city people moved to the country. It was like a game. Some of these city people . . . now were trekking back" (299). These people include the Baldwins, and *American Beauty* finally takes a sharp turn from im-ages of downtrodden farms and declining families to finish on a forward-looking note and a Ferber message of the promise of mixture, no matter how turbulent the process. True, the old New Englander—albeit one who was not sufficiently elevated to sit near the Oakes pew—returns to Con-necticut to save the house. With the romantic prospect of Candace mar-rying the handsome Orrange, Ferber's message of mixture as vigor and promise emerges, minus the traumatic endings of racial bloodshed in *Cimarron*. The gothic, misshapen Oakes legacy has vanished, replaced by the handsome hybrid cultivar of American beauty. The new union fulfills Orrange's comment to his mother of the family's Oakes blood: "'It ran so thin after two hundred years that there wasn't any blood left. . . . I'm pretty good, with Ondy's blood in me, and yours'" (280–81). The Polish blood, simultaneously despised and needed, provides the only potential for the maintenance of the prized Oakes house and, by extension, the Connecticut Yankee.

Come and Get It takes the ethnic tension of Kipling's "outside invasion" articulated in *American Beauty* and moves it west. Ferber continued to interrogate gradations of whiteness, and the ways in which each ethnic or national subculture embodies and diverges from the stereotypes sur-rounding it. The West, as in *Cimarron*, offers a potent template because of the relative novelty of its cities, towns, and social taxonomies. The 1934 novel focuses on a family whose robber-baron fortune is made in lumbering, exploring the strain on the land itself along with the social points of pressure involved in harvesting wood. In *Come and Get It*, saving the land requires Ferber's own alchemy of ethnicities, including hardy Swedish lumberjacks who intermarry with the landowning Scotch-Irish gentry. Class mobility owes more to determination and blended blood than to original station, and Ferber exposes anew the evanescent and often arbitrary nature of social assignment that both confines and liberates her characters.

Some audiences adored *Come and Get It*. Positioned as Ferber's final stroke of the American regional compass (counting *Show Boat* as a southern story), *Come and Get It* takes Ferber to the Wisconsin Northwoods. "[A] clean chapter from Americana!" wrote Betty Brainerd. "It promises to be the book of the year. It deserves the Pulitzer prize." Brainerd was so smitten that she launched into Ferberish diction: "it is an epic—a saga of the Middle West woods done sometimes in pastels, sometimes in rugged, bold strokes, and so artistically blended that you hardly know where the pastels end and the rugged strokes begin" (1935). But others saw it is a flop. "Miss Ferber has not carried it off," wrote John Chamberlain in the *New York Times*. "[A]s good thought and good writing, Miss Ferber's novel is simply not there. It sounds like . . . the section that is stuffed between two sets of more realistic dossiers as a warning of how not to write enduring fiction." Yet even Chamberlain understood where Ferber's greatest impact lay: "The three generations from shirtsleeves to shirtsleeves motif, which proves, among other things, that the heart of America is still sound" (1935, 17). Regardless of opinion on each work, Ferber's role as American portraitist remained clear. What does not come across in these trade reviews, although they understand Ferber's focus on class mobility—shirtsleeves-to-shirtsleeves—is the complex ways in which race and whiteness inform the text.

Barney "Gusto" Glasgow, a Scotch-Irish lumberjack who becomes "the Paul Bunyan of the region" (*Come and Get It* [1934], 71), is the novel's progenitor. Barney's father dies heroically, and the boy is raised in the timber camp's kitchen, feeding his fellow woodsmen and fending for himself when his mother also dies. The camp provides a particularly wide array of ethnicities, including "Frenchmen, Irishmen, English, and Scotch, Indians and Scandinavians" (77), as well as "Finns and Swedes and Danes, Canucks and Germans, French and Indians" (102). The nearby town is filled with an even more varied range, and a longer Ferber list: "French, Swedes, Scotch, Irish. . . . The Cornishmen who worked in the iron mines, and the Poles and the Italians too" (117). Ferber writes that "certain Cornish words crept into the North Country language and became fixed there. The Swedes and Irish began to use them, all unconsciously" (118). Blending occurs without knowledge, while the ethnic groups remain self-identified, down to the Cornishmen, a sub-subculture with its own name and recognition. Ferber's rendition of this heterogeneously backgrounded group recalls the true "melting pot" image, with "creeping" words leading to "unconscious" language shifts, a predictor that earlier identities will be lost and the hyphens elided once all the are "Americans."

Despite these intimations of mixing, however, the taxonomy persists, exemplified by a joke making the rounds of the town: "so this lad says, 'What the hell is Thanksgiving Day, I never heard tell of it?' So Conlin speaks up and says, 'Damn if I know, it's some kind of a Protestant day, I guess'" (121). With ignorance of something so blatantly American and related to the heralded New England of *American Beauty* as Thanksgiving, which is then translated into "something Protestant" by the presumably Irish-Catholic Conlin, Ferber demonstrates how the culture of the midwestern logging camps relies upon the mosaic of backgrounds. Descriptors and names meld and swirl until they are almost meaningless, as when Ferber writes that the camp cook was a "slant-eyed Finn whom the jacks called Chink" (94). In this hubbub of ethnonyms and national origins, physical markers are still available—but they do not necessarily apply to the seemingly appropriate individual.

Out of this combustible grouping appear the two men who most look after Barney, couched resolutely in their own ethnicities: "Tom Melendy, the sentimental Irishman," and "Swan Bostrom, the hard-headed Swede" (90). Although Swan is years older than Barney, he takes a servant's approach to his friend: "'You be my boss yet,'" (100), he says, and promptly makes it true. Barney also accepts this role and succeeds in social ascent because he "had come of good stock. . . . He was Scotch-Irish-American—

purposeful, sturdy, ruthless" (97). Invested in his preeminence at the top
of the ethnicity scale, Barney believes that his heritage renders him fit to
leave, just as Swan envisions himself as rightfully placed as a Swedish servant. Notably, of the characters in the woods, only Barney's background
is described with the last Deweyesque hyphenation as "American"—at
least when he prospers. In his weaker moments, such as when he falls
in love with Swan's wife Lotta, "All his Scotch firmness left him, and his
Irish sentimentality possessed him" (107). Lotta, a "professional prostitute turned housewife," comes from a mixed background: "Porty'gese and
her father a Finlander" (131), the presumed stem of her unusual physicality: a combination of blonde hair and black eyes, upon which her many
admirers remark.

Drawn to Lotta, Barney nevertheless sets his sights on a more financially rewarding and socially elevating match. Presented with the lumber company's owner's mansion, "it was as though he had been all his
life accustomed to it. 'I've got good blood in me. . . . That's why,'" he
thinks (112). This "good blood" predisposes him to be "responsive to material delights" (1). Barney pays for these desires by marrying the owner's
daughter for status rather than love. Their marriage represents a rectify-
ing of Barney's "good blood" with his financial status. Just like the operagoers in *The Girls,* Barney achieves rapid mobility. "In the amazing American way he had jumped two generations" (60), writes Ferber, because
Barney can wear a dinner coat "with ease," and "had learned to pick a
wine with his dinner" (60).

In the town of Butte des Morts which the lumber company owns—
the "hill of the dead" name echoing Barney's loveless marriage and the
suffocating taxonomy as well as reflecting a lake with the same name
in Wisconsin, local stratification locks Polish people at the bottom. The
girls who work in the mill are "Polish and Bohemian, most of them,"
and they have a "curious clay gray" complexion (35), reminiscent of the
sheety-white paper-mill girls in Herman Melville's anti-industrial 1855
short story "The Paradise of Bachelors and the Tarturus of Maids." Their
work is physically perilous, as an employee reports: "'One of those Polack girls at the guillotine sliced a finger and they're afraid it will have to
come off'" (41). The Polish women's bodies are viewed as disposable in a

world in which losing a finger in the machinery is part of the day's work. As paper is manufactured, the girls come unmade.

With its sweeping classifications and characterizations, *Come and Get It* bore real-world ramifications for Ferber because it infuriated some Polish American readers. When the novel was serialized in the *Women's Home Companion* in 1934, Ferber had originally used the term "Polack" and named one of the less appealing mill workers "Gussie Pulaski." A reader named H. J. Kubiak wrote in to say that Pulaski was the name of an American hero—Casimir Pulaski, who reportedly saved George Washington's life during the Revolutionary War—and that "I can assure you that every one of the four million Polish-Americans will feel keenly this brazen insult to his racial dignity" (Letter to Edna Ferber [1934], 1). The references were altered when the novel was printed in its entirety. The episode proved both Ferber's influence—people cared if she seemed to demean their ethnicity—and her reinstatement of ethnic stereotypes even as she wrote stories that posited to disentangle presuppositions about certain groups.

While these contested workers are largely Polish, the overseers at Barney's paper mill themselves are ethnically mixed, "originally from New England, many of them. . . . [T]hey had married into the families of Wisconsin European-born settlers, and their sons and daughters had intermarried, so that now you found Polish names and German and Dutch mingling with the older New England nomenclature" (49). Mimicking the trajectory of *American Beauty*'s True Baldwin, who moves to Chicago after his Connecticut upbringing, and hearkening back to Selina DeJong's astonishment at the name changes in Chicago in *So Big*, these "intermarried" Americans make up the higher social levels of the town, showing a progression from Polish, German, or Dutch to "mingle" with the New England patrician bloodlines.

The products of this "mingling" collide with Barney's carefully plotted ascent and reign, highlighting the misalignment between his years of living with blue-blooded Emma Louise and the "vitality" borne of his heritage. The disjointedness catches up with Barney when he falls in love with Swan's beautiful granddaughter, Lotta, also the granddaughter of the original Lotta. (The names in this novel are simply doubled, without differing nicknames or diminutives.) The novel takes a turn toward the girl-on-the-swing model of the Gilded Age—Emma Louise "knew of Stanford White" (319), the famous architect killed by the jealous husband of his young mistress, Evelyn Nesbit. Barney attempts to find legitimate ways to keep Lotta nearby. As Barney becomes increasingly wealthy and rapacious, he puts his own father-in-law's similarly avaricious behavior behind him: "He forgot about Jed Hewitt and the land-grabbing and the homesteaders . . . the ravishing of his own country. He thought of himself, now, as a fine and patriotic citizen" (184). Ferber's elision of the sexually charged word "ravishment" with appropriating the land demonstrates that Lotta and the woods his paper company destroys are merged for Barney, who considers his consumption "patriotic," as he tries to take what he wants as he pleases, using his considerable financial power to do so.

Layered on top of Barney's vexed relationship with Lotta is a current of Swedish stereotypes and attributions so thick that a habit Ferber attributes to Emma Louise—"She had never thought highly of her husband's boyhood friend. She referred to him as that Swede" (224)—seems to fit the novel itself more aptly. Swedishness accounts for myriad features. Swan is relentlessly described with an ethnic tinge, such as how he "[c]lung with characteristic Swedish tenacity" (186) or how "[t]he old Swede's eyes were as trusting as a faithful dog's" (192). He even has "white Swedish lashes" (204). To attempt to allay any comprehension of how he truly feels about Lotta, Barney attempts to belittle her with the comment that "[s]he's a little Swede girl from up north" (327). Ethnicity intercedes at all levels: when he restrains himself around Lotta, Barney attributes it to his "canny Scotch ancestry," as if the same shrewdness that brought him richness accounts for his rectitude (290). Even once he is firmly ensconced in moneyed comfort, Barney's ethnic classification continues to define him—even to himself. The innate nature of background cannot be surmounted.

Evvy, Barney's daughter, commits to a similarly loveless marriage to ensure her continued ease. History is set to repeat itself—a favorite Ferber plot device along with the redoubled names—when she is engaged to the unappealing Orville Bremmer, in a marriage that "was Butte des Morts paper-mill royalty marrying Butte des Morts paper-mill sub-royalty" (19). Engaged to dull, wealthy Orville, Evvy still sleeps with handsome Polish laborer Tony Schwerke. She defends herself to her father: "'What were you but a smart lumberjack! Well, Tony Schwerke's a smart mill hand" (215). Despite the candor of this comment—and the uncomfortable likening of his daughter's lover to himself—Barney considers confronting Tony. Regarding his paper, Barney says, "'Good white stock'" (222). With this double-edged comment he seems to reassure himself that Evvy should marry the anemic but wealthy Orvie and produce more "good white stock" instead of half-Polish children. With the awkward understanding that Barney knows of his and Evvy's relationship, Schwerke offers to leave, but "All the Irish in him, all the sentiment in him, rushed to the fore" (222). Barney tells him to stay, condoning the relationship and the ethnic diversion, recognizing its appeal and furthering Ferber's understanding of mixture as healthy.

With his own attempted illicit relationship, however, Barney deals with someone far less obliging in Lotta. Karie describes her daughter: "'I guess the Finn and the Portygee . . . I guess they must have melted together and then got hard as a lump in Lotta . . . a real ambitious girl'" (292). Ethnic mixture breeds vitality. Lotta's shrewd and calculating "ambition" ensures her survival, according to Karie. The questionable but tenacious heritage seems to have skipped the altogether-Swedish-affiliated Karie and gone straight to the second dark-eyed Lotta. Lotta desires not Barney, however, but his son Bernie. Reacting to this shock, Barney relies upon ethnically and class-based insults to abuse the young couple, calling Lotta a "'Swede dish-washer'" and a "'big Swede waitress'" (316). Scorned, Barney relies upon Lotta's ethnic heritage to provide insults rather than invite attraction. In his jealous hysteria, Barney kills himself, a pregnant Evvy, Emma Louise, and Orville when he drops a match leading to a boat explosion, and with his death (which Ferber regretted) it is almost as if another book begins, as the novel's focus shifts to Lotta's inability to blend in to Butte des Morts society. "In [*Come and Get It*] I committed a serious error," Ferber writes in *A Peculiar Treasure*. "A little more than halfway through the book I killed the character called Barney Glasgow, and with his death the backbone of the book was broken. He was the most vital and engaging person in the story" (1939, 372).

Ferber's use of the word "vital" for Barney both suggests his vibrant personality and the necessity of his character. Yet as the novel soldiers on, the less lively but still alive Glasgows continue to hack their way through contemporary society, without Barney but still very much with the ethnic framing he inhabited and delineated. Others thwart them: Scotty, Barney's driver, attempts to murder Lotta, whom he blames for Barney's death. Scotty's identity is remarkable only for its short reach—he is Canadian—but his character is in the mold of Jot and other Ferber dwarves, with a "Quilpish" body that refers to Dickens's *Old Curiosity Shop* villain, and underlines his peculiarity and mendacity (1934, 25). Other characters lack Scotty's venality but internalize the Glasgows' struggle. For one, while Barney finds no trouble jumping social class to marry into paper-mill royalty, the rules differ for women. Lotta's thwarted assimilation raises questions of American class mobility and definition. Lou Shifty, Lotta's African American maid, appears briefly but understands these constraints. "'I'm itchin' to fix [your hair] next time you go to a pahty, all puff's here to here, an' a han'some a-gret ornament, you'd pass for a queen" (344), she tells Lotta. With this comment, Lou not only demonstrates that she knows about her employer's frustrated desire to appear in society, but also pointedly enunciates what Lotta is attempting: to pass as a patrician matron when she is truly a "Swede dish-washer."

Unwanted by both high- and low-caste residents of Butte des Morts, "Step by step Lotta pulled herself up on the crazy ladder that was America's social structure" (351), Ferber writes. She and Karie move to New York, where "[t]he War had created a careless camaraderie. Social barriers had slipped to the vanishing point" (408). Lotta hires a woman named Rachel Penny, who "'can get anybody into society,'" a forerunner of Mrs. Coventry Bellop in *Saratoga Trunk* (412). Rachel—an embodiment of "the crazy ladder"—charges $25,000 to render an individual socially viable. Impressed by Karie's plain-spoken ways, Rachel advises Lotta: "'Listen, Mrs. Glasgow, don't you let her get away, this mother of yours. Salty. They'll love it'" (420). In a performance-conscious way—the "'They'll love it'" refers to an audience and an actor, as if Karie's earthiness is somehow created—Ferber's meta-textual analysis of Karie alerts the reader to her value. With her constant references to Swedishness and the lumber-camp restaurant where she and Lotta worked, Karie grounds *Come and Get It* in its origins and maintains the most honest, straightforward ethnic line throughout, keeping Swedishness at the forefront. In fact, another character tells Lotta that "'[t]he old girl's a character. You wouldn't believe her if you met in her in a book.'" (424). With this wink, Ferber acknowledges the exaggeration of her characters. America, she seems to say with these outsize individuals, defies belief.

Lotta's relocation to London brings new awareness of home, including a representation of African Americanness that enlarges upon the narrowly defined image of Lou Shifty, and adds another dimension to the question of categories in the Wisconsin ethnic economy, so tightly bound by Swedish and other white ethnicities. Abroad, "even royalty danced to frantic jazz in hot little boxes called night clubs, where aristocratic sweat mingled with the exudations of the frenetic negro orchestra. Aristocracy came off second best, for the musicians were only acting. There was about them an inner secret dignity, a gently sardonic acceptance of life no matter how brutal. Even a night club could not penetrate the deeps of an American-born negro" (423).

The image of the African American "deeps" as well as the musicians "only acting" suggests a double-consciousness that begins with Lou Shifty's own nuanced understanding of Lotta's precarious position. This passage also points up Lotta's preoccupation with social status, as Ferber underlines its ludicrous nature. Not only does "even royalty" dance in these confined night clubs, aristocratic merit is erased by the jazz musicians' lack of sincerity as they play. While the patrician white British dance—with all evident sincerity—to the "frantic" music, the musicians themselves are "only acting." *Come and Get It* is preoccupied with failed performance, particularly in the case of Lotta's attempt at being a version of an American aristocrat. Only the jazz musicians maintain human dignity, ironically through acting, leaving the aristocrats "second-best." On foreign soil, the African Americans are positioned as inscrutable, but also as faring better than their royal audiences, a notion Ferber gestured toward in *So Big* with her mentions of jazz musicians and picks up in the 1939 short story "Nobody's in Town," which features an African American musician named Lacy, whose music is destined to be played all over the world, "and the red plush boxes were to shout bravos at the lank limp black man who so lackadaisically came out to take his bow" (1939, 60).

In other words, Lacy, like the jazz musicians in *Come and Get It,* will be accepted, paid, and applauded by the rich. Their talent can transcend class even if their ethnicity leaves them at the bottom of the social ladder.

Ending with a look toward the future, *Come and Get It* follows the family for one more generation, continuing to chronicle the expatriate life with Bernie and Lotta's twins, Bard and Dina (both named, of course, after Barney, although dark-complected Dina favors her great-grandmother Lotta, with "the old Portygee cropping out'" (503). While the two are raised in Europe, they profess love for America and their great-grandfather Swan, preferring "Iron Ridge better than any place in the world." This guileless profession demonstrates the purity and authenticity of the youngest generation, which looks toward its hyphenated heritage, but stays connected to its American present (430). Another like-named descendant of an earlier character, the young Tom Melendy, writes a book called *"The Rape of the American Forest"* decrying the culture of the lumberjack that made Barney and Jed Hewitt before him so wealthy in the first place (433). While Barney sees his ability to turn the forest into money as an American act, Tom's novel demonstrates the reverse by giving voice to Americans who want to preserve the actual American topography. With these echoes of their forefathers represented literally in their namesakes, Ferber shows the promise of youth, and the idea that they can look backward and forward, so that the mixture of Swede and Scotch-Irish "American" finally comes to fruition.

Fittingly, after the crash of 1929, Karie leads the multigenerational procession home. Bard calls their home country "'romantic and swell and American'" (469). He and his sister seek to discover America as anthropologists and disenfranchised patriots, and as they travel, Dina encounters her own version of the jazz musicians in England: "'There is a train maid, a negress, she's quite beautiful with a Madonna face, she says she lives in Harlem. I told her I'd heard all about it and that I'd rather see it than any place in America except Hollywood. I asked her if it really was as orgiastic as they say it is, but she said I had the wrong idea entirely, she belongs to a very dignified family'" (473).

Dina's patronizing understanding of Harlem links the area with "orgiastic" behavior and with Hollywood, a place built on performance. She would "rather" see Harlem, a desire she voices moments after demanding pie à la mode, as if she wants to consume America, from its food to its people. Just as Barney ravishes the forests, the twins move in to consume the American culture they have been denied. They are poised to "come and get it," and in what constitutes both a reversal and a reiteration of their family's previous experiences, Bard and Dina relive the immigrant experience in their own way. While their mother seeks escape from American class assignment, her children return to turn her presumptions upside down as much as the "topsy-turvy" (435) British society that literally stands Lotta on her head during an outlandish health phase.

History repeats itself—again—when Dina takes up with the young Tony Schwerke. Yet this youngest generation, without the prohibition of a higher-class Scotch-Irish descendant marrying a lower-class Polish one, can remedy the earlier cataclysm. The younger couple inherits the potential to fix the future with their mingled ethnicities. Mixture validates their relationship and lends promise to the future, which appears auspicious for these young people, who wax tirelessly about their country. Tom says, "'This is the most vital, amazing, stirring, goofy, thrilling country in the whole world, and I care about it in a Big Way'" (498), while Dina adds "'It's alive here. It's crazy and upset and cock-eyed and whirling, but it's alive'" (504).

This "alive" or "vital" place is pressured by points of intersection with historic and ethnically vexed moments. Tom says: "Sometimes I get sick and fed up with [America], and then along comes the Sacco-Vanzetti thing, or those Scottsboro boys . . . thousands of men and women willing to give time and energy and their very lives—for what! To try to get justice for a couple of Wops and a bunch of hobo nigger boys" (500). The Irish American Tom seems to use these slurs to provoke his audience and make a point about the righteousness of activists who participate in social causes such as charged Communists Sacco and Vanzetti or the Scottsboro teenagers accused of rape. He acknowledges a great shift—"for what!"—and sees an idealized future of social activism, where "men and women" who are presumably of mixed backgrounds address injustice together. Not every character embraces Tom's galvanizing rhetoric, but the message of change infuses the novel. When Lotta chances to meet Rachel Penny, the social climbing advisor, as a middle-aged woman, Rachel compliments her on her appearance: "'Good peasant stock. Nothing like it'" (507). In *Come and Get It*, wholesomeness lies in ethnic mixture and lower-class status.

In *American Beauty*, Ferber relies upon extreme imagery to overturn preexisting ideas of the halcyon Puritan New England. With visions of unearthly, spectral characters and events, the novel delves far into gothic territory before emerging with a complex, yet ultimately auspicious, recipe for a vigorously mixed society, promising a future for New England to rival the strength of its past. With *Come and Get It*, Ferber pushed into the future, both in terms of westering and her vision for the next generation of hybrid Americans. For Ferber, overly refined environments spoil both people and the country, and only the latest, best-blended generation can salvage America. The family returns to the woods, with an aged Swan mistaking Bard for his old friend Gusto. As in *American Beauty*, the circle closes. But *Come and Get It*'s message lies in its frantic assessment of a forward-looking country that must continually revivify with a meticulously adjusted alchemy of individual and societal ethnicities.

6

PASSING FANCY
Saratoga Trunk

GRAVE TOPICS WERE ON FERBER'S MIND as she wrote her 1941 novel *Saratoga Trunk*. Although its Gilded Age New Orleans and Saratoga settings are worlds away from the troubles of the Second World War, the book followed on the heels of *A Peculiar Treasure*, a soul-searching study investigating Ferber's Jewishness and its effect on her writing. Ferber dedicated *A Peculiar Treasure* to Adolf Hitler, "who has made me a better Jew and a more understanding and tolerant human being" (1939, 291). Also, her other 1941 effort was "No Room at the Inn: A Story of Christmas in the World Today," a short story set in World War II Germany in which a Jewish couple named Joe and Mary are loaded into a filthy train car headed to an uncertain fate. Mary eventually gives birth in a ditch, and names the baby Niemand, or "nobody." A German soldier asks, "'That the best you can do for him! . . . Jesus! . . . Well, cheer up, he's a fine-looking boy. He might grow up to be quite a kid, at that'" (24). With this heavy-handed parable, Ferber reminded readers that every Jew dying in Germany could have been Jesus. She was using broad strokes for large topics.

Contemporary reviewers saw *Saratoga Trunk*, however, as worlds away from the serious kind of writing that Ferber put forth in her autobiography or "No Room at the Inn." They acknowledged that Ferber would have another best seller on her hands (which she did), but as Ralph Thompson wrote in the *New York Times,* "All that Hollywood will have to supply is a camera and unexposed film . . . no dillydallying about character development, chronology, or such subtleties." Others agreed: *Saratoga Trunk* was superficial and stagey.

Although *Saratoga Trunk* is admittedly one of Ferber's more thespian novels—and she did, in fact, first envision it as a play—its themes are complex and far thornier than its rollicking pace would indicate. (The "trunk" in the title refers to a branch railroad line to Binghamton, New York, on the Delaware and Hudson rivers.) Its topics are not too far from some of those she tackled in *A Peculiar Treasure* and "No Room at the Inn," and Ferber's treatment of complicated and complicating questions of race and ethnicity push the novel beyond a series of madcap adventures. Many of the Saratoga episodes, including a conflagration at a railroad depot and a fixed horse-race, bear little relevance to the initial discussions about racial and class performance with which the book begins. But this central series of hijinks is bracketed by two episodes that prove vexed contemplations on ethnicity and the shifting and shifty nature of American social structure.

Saratoga Trunk uses its careening plot to emphasize the extreme nature of the mercurial and vivid Clio Dulaine, the novel's heroine, the granddaughter of a woman of color and the daughter of a Creole man named Nicolas Dulaine and his mistress, Rita. Clio's disruptive character, in turn, emphasizes the lack of stability in the society she attempts to ascend in her quest to wed well. Clio, an admittedly screen-ready heroine with her beauty and charm, surmounts a societally challenged admixture of blood and station to become a reigning figure in Saratoga's stratified American society. Clio proves she can cross boundaries, choosing her own station in life. In doing so, she demonstrates the artificiality of race and class structures, although she herself vows to appear Creole—which she figures as white, European, and aristocratic—and respectable. With the help of her two acolytes and a dashing escort to cloak the power and wiles she possesses in a society that prizes apparent helplessness in women, she navigates financial and social success. Clio creates a role for herself without the burden of honesty.

Clio's decisions concerning when to hide her ethnicity and when to play with it recall Fanny's, but while Fanny feels ashamed of pretending not to be Jewish, Clio never gives a thought to demoting her heritage of color in order to rise. The qualities to which the novel ascribes her success— her vigorously mixed ethnic and social heritage—are those she wishes to deny in order to achieve her longed-for life of financial ease and status.

Bound as Clio is to climb to the top of Saratoga's social ladder, Ferber consistently undermines any hierarchy left standing for longer than a chapter or two. One leading dowager, Mrs. Coventry Bellop, seems at first like a comfortable widow who has earned the right to stay at Saratoga for the season. But, as she tells Clio, she is actually living hand-to-mouth on her ability to manipulate society, matchmaking and selling family secrets, much like Rachel Penny, the penniless but blooded Londoner who tries to help Lottie in *Come and Get It*. The mainstay, and most snobbish member, of the Saratoga clique was a waitress in her youth. "'It doesn't pay to inquire too closely into the background of us Saratoga summer folks,'" one matron says (1941, 223). The whole society is built on sand, and yet Clio still turns to subterfuge to conquer it and achieve her dream of a rich husband. She rails against a confining system with no substance, but simultaneously depends upon it to elevate her. Throughout the novel, Clio's background is described as illicit or murky, alluding to the somewhat for-hire nature of her dead mother's relationship to her father as well as Clio's African American heritage. Clio's mother Rita is a *placée*, the partly African American mistress of a Creole man. Her childhood is clouded by a tragedy: the death by pistol of her father in her mother's bedroom. After his death, the Dulaine family exiles Rita, and Clio is raised in France by her mother along with her aunt, "the hearty shrewd strumpet Belle Piquery" (36), and a devoted staff.

A New Orleans background itself, of course, evokes the idea of mixture since the city itself is famous for its many cultures and generally outlandish feel. Ferber writes that the city has the "smell of an old and carnal city, of a worldly and fascinating city" (40). Although raised in Paris, Clio is every bit a product of New Orleans, through her mother and aunt's stories and memories. At home in Louisiana, they occupy marginal positions that are part of the fabric of the place. "Though these women belonged to that strange and exotic stratum which was the New Orleans underworld, Rita's life had for many years been intertwined with that of one of the city's oldest and most aristocratic of families. . . . [S]he was queen of that half-world peopled by women of doubtful blood" (14), writes Ferber.

"Strange," "exotic," "half-world," "doubtful"—Ferber's language points to Clio's inheritance of mystery and casts her in the same mold that the tragic mulatta figure initiated in nineteenth-century American literature, and that Ferber continued in *Show Boat*. Authors traditionally signal that a character is a tragic mulatta through physical features, such as Clotel's "glossy ringlets of raven hair" (111) in William Wells Brown's 1853 novel *Clotel*. Clio, for her part, has black hair, "dark and thick and winged" eyebrows, "naturally creamy" skin, and "darker" eyes (1941, 59), as well as "an unusual glow tinting the creamy pallor of her cheeks" (32). Clio uses white powder as a cosmetic solution to passing, applying it so thickly that it resembles a "clown's mask, except for its beauty" (59). Clio uses her mixed background to offer mystery and feminine appeal, even as she powders herself white. She stands as a true foil to the tragic mulatta as a woman of color who passes for white in the dominant society, but she also plays with the tricky nature of ethnicity politics in her relentless recasting of her identity.[1]

Clio's singing—both her voice and her choice of song—encapsulates her blended origins. She sings a "true mixture of music—music she had heard at the Paris Opera; songs that Rita Dulaine had hummed in a sweet and melancholy tremolo; plantation songs, Negro spirituals, folk songs with which Kaka had sung her to sleep in her childhood; songs that Aunt Belle Piquery had sung in a shrill off-key soprano, risqué songs whose origins had been the brothels and gambling houses of the New Orleans of her heyday" (31).[2] The sound of Clio's "true mixture" is a "rich, true contralto" (31), which stands in opposition to her mother's "melancholy" and her aunt's "shrill" voices. Descriptions of African American and illicit influence, from spirituals to bawdy-house tunes, pervade her music along with those from the opera, so that Clio becomes a product of her

1. *Saratoga Trunk* seems to have a relationship with that other book about a southern woman who succeeds at all costs. *Gone With the Wind* was published five years earlier, and there are moments when Ferber seems to borrow from Mitchell's book when she tells about the South, from the older African American woman who has her belle's suitor figured out from the beginning to the woman who embodies mixture and takes on the world. Even the euphonious given names, Clint and Clio seem to echo Scarlett and Rhett. In her biography of Ferber, however, Julie Gilbert recalls that Ferber did not recognize Vivien Leigh, even when she (Gilbert) said, "Oh, Aunt Edna. . . . If you couldn't remember Vivien Leigh, at least you could have remembered Scarlett O'Hara." She turned to me with a bleary eye. "'Who?' she asked" (1978, 145). In the same volume, however, Gilbert includes a photograph of Ferber in front of an old mansion, which she had playfully inscribed "Edna O'Ferber."

2. Magnolia, of course, also sings African American songs that she has been taught.

raising, with her songs giving voice to her identity. Although these same combinations produced less effective voices in her exiled mother and aunt, Clio's return to America represents an opportunity for the blend of ethnic and class components to succeed.

Like her songs, Clio's "bizarre attendants who walk in her wake" (40) echo her in all her difference. Cupidon, Clio's coachman and manservant, resembles other Ferber dwarves such as Jot in *American Beauty* and Scotty in *Come and Get It*. He is a child-man character to whom Clio tosses table scraps. "The large head, the powerful arms and chest belonged to a dwarf, a little man not three feet high. . . . He might have been any age, fifteen, twenty, thirty, forty" (17). Like Clio's, Cupidon's identity evades definition. He sleeps outside Clio's door as a sort of combination factotum and lapdog. Also like Clio, he confuses onlookers with his resistance to conform to any one standard: "'Sometimes you talk like a nigger bootblack and sometimes you talk like a character in a book,' one tells him (200). He and his mistress invoke a combination of perplexity and attraction.

Kakaracou, whose real name is Angelique Pluton and whom Clio calls Kaka, is Clio's mainstay, a sort of combination housekeeper, lady's maid, and nurse, whose identity rivals Clio's for blending. She "spoke a curious jargon, a mixture of French, Spanish, New Orleans colloquialisms, African Negro" (15). Her skin "was neither black nor coffee-colored but the shade of a ripe fig, purplish dusted with gray" (16), and appears "at once vaguely Egyptian, New Orleans Negro duenna, and a figure out of the Arabian Nights" (40), Ferber writes. Her language and appearance are plural, as Ferber piles on descriptors that only serve to evade definition. Ferber preempts any assumptions readers may make about Kaka's race— she is *not* "black," *not* "coffee-colored"—and threatens any preconceived ideas about Kaka as a traditional mammy figure. Indeed, she refuses to be called a mammy. "'It is a thing I hate. Out of the slave days,'" she says (90). Kaka is every bit as complicated a character as Clio, with eyes that "had the sad yet compassionate quality found in an old race whose heritage is tragedies remembered" (40). This heritage is, of course, Clio's as well, and in her constant reminders to Clio of her non-Creole background, Kaka also reminds Clio of the similarity between mistress and servant. Kaka, who dabbles in voodoo, claims that Clio is bewitched, but that the witch powder she gave her has done no good because "'Miss Clio

she a witch woman herself'" (142). The three—Clio, Kaka, and Cupide—
form their own society, with its own language. "Not alone Kaka, but Clio
and Cupide were adept in these lingual gymnastics. They were given
to talking among themselves in a spicy *ragout* of French, English, and
Gombo that was almost unintelligible to an outsider" (71). The three
of them share the sole aim to elevate Clio, who, for her part, "actually
achieved the Protean role" (55).

Clio decides to pass as a respectable white woman, vowing that she
will be different from Rita and Belle Piquery, who accept both their assigned roles as prostitute and mistress, and their exile after Nicolas's
death. "Hearing her reminiscing thus, one would have thought her a descendant of a long line of Louisiana aristocrats rather than the woman
she really was. The formality of marriage had not been part of her lineage.
. . . Rita Dulaine had emerged from this murky background as a water lily
lifts its creamy petals out of the depths of a muddy pond" (19). The water
lily image of cleanliness on filth, reminiscent of the magnolia-petal cliché
that was traditionally overused to describe white southern women's skin
as well as Magnolia Ravenal in *Show Boat,* reverses the societal direction
of Rita and Belle's status as kept woman and prostitute. Rita uses the surname Dulaine, underlining her place as Nicolas Dulaine's mistress, and
although Ferber describes the women as from a "murky" background,
Rita is nevertheless positioned as clean, fresh, and bright, something that
will bolster her descendant's efforts to become a rich man's wife.

Rita's ownership of the borderline respectability of the placée, the sort
of legitimized mistress who is housed and cared for by the Creole man,
does not placate Clio. Her mother tells her of the *garçonniere* planned
when she was born, a place where a mistress could comfortably raise the
illegitimate children (presumably boys) of her lover. Clio desires a higher
station in life than that of a placée or prostitute, telling her aunt that she
will be "quite, quite respectable. Not like you" (21). America offers Clio
the place to perform this social ascension. When Clio taunts her aunt
with her position as a Dulaine, Belle reminds her that her grandmother
was a free woman of color. "'You and Mama aren't Dulaines,'" Clio counters. "'I am. My life's going to be different. I shan't be a fool about men.
They'll be fools about me'" (22). Indeed, Clio bawls her Dulaine origins
to the world, although Kaka, like Belle Piquery, unerringly reminds her

she is not solely Creole. "In private she never missed an opportunity to remind the girl that her origin was one-half aristocratic Creole and one-half new Orleans underworld. . . . Yet, 'I am!' Clio shouted now. 'I'm Creole!'" Upon seeing Nicolas Dulaine's bloodstains on the bedroom floor where he was shot, Kaka is horrified, but Clio strokes the spot, in a weirdly literal adoration of her father's bloodline reminiscent of Tamar Oakes's gothic worship of her heritage in *American Beauty*. "'His blood. My blood. They are the same. I love it, this spot" (29). She sleeps in the room, the stain uncleaned.

With her mother and aunt dead, and nothing more than the women's stories of their old home to go on, Clio, Kaka, and Cupide embark upon a plan to blackmail the Dulaine family in New Orleans in order to fund Clio's debut in "respectable" society. They move from Paris back to Rampart Street and undertake the renovation of Rita's house, in "the neighborhood that had about it something flavorous, something faintly sinister, something shoddy, something of past dignity" (69). Ferber's superficial sketch of the post-Reconstruction South of New Orleans serves to underline Clio's identity, which has the "faintly sinister" death of her father in its background, as well as the "past dignity" of her Creole heritage. Kaka reprimands her to "take shame on yourself, denying your own mama" (36) by privileging her Dulaine half, but Clio lays down the law with her servants: "'Then remember that no matter what I say I am—that I am. I shall be what it suits me to be'" (37). In one way, blood is everything to Clio. She clings to her father's blood and his aristocratic Creole past as the key to the societal elevation she craves. At the same time, it is her mixed origins that give her the strength to come up with new and vital identities. "The girl herself had the face of an actress, inherited from that other Clio who had come to New Orleans in 1791, one of a homeless refugee band of players who had fled the murderous Negro uprising in the French West Indies" (19), Ferber writes. The heritage of the actress of color gives Clio the skill and power to pass for white if and when she chooses.

Clint Maroon, the first man to be a fool about Clio is, like her, a bit of a grifter. She vows to marry a rich and respectable someone else with his help (Clint vows to be the best man at her wedding), which leads to the let's-put-on-a-show-in-the-barn aspect of the plot. As anyone who has seen a Hollywood movie can attest, these two will clearly end up together.

Clint, a white Texan, is described as mixed in terms of gender identification. "Curiously soft-voiced and rather drawling for so big and full-blooded a man," Clint is a blend of well-clothed delicacy and hyper-masculinity, fist-fighting and wearing embroidered cravats with equal abandon. Like many Ferber duos—Bick and Leslie Benedict in *Giant,* Gaylord and Magnolia Ravenal in *Show Boat*—Clint and Clio are "almost incredibly handsome" (3) and attract attention at every age; the novel opens with the pair still drawing admiring glances well into their eighties.

"Adventurers, both of them, bent on cracking the shell of the world that was to be their oyster" (75), Ferber writes. Clint, however, becomes more than a mirror to Clio. He becomes a lens through which to view her paradoxical nature. Just as her ethnicity remains fluid, so does her personality, including her gendered performances. "'Say, what kind of woman are you anyway! . . . Sometimes she seemed an innocent girl; sometimes an accomplished courtesan'" (77) he says. Ultimately, these conflicting roles lead to defeminization in Clint's eyes. "It's like being with a man sometimes," he says (101).

Even though Kaka accuses her of "play-acting" (another jibe at Clio's elision of her mother's influence, and a reference to her actress forebear), Clio sticks to her self-created role as a French countess, duping New Orleanians who thrill to see her and her handsome escort at the opera and restaurants around town. "Ignoring the coded systems of racial mixing and segregation followed by generations of her female forbears, she capitalizes on the American infatuation with aristocracy by inventing an entirely new identity," Donna Campbell writes (2003, 35).

Eventually, Clio extracts ten thousand dollars from the Dulaines in exchange for leaving New Orleans and the scandal behind. Next, she insists upon physically destroying the house she had worked so hard to renovate, believing its removal will add dignity to her mother's memory. This making and unmaking of the house on Rampart Street reflects her demolition and repair of her various identities. Ferber's descriptions of Cupide's role in the destruction reflect the constant sense of the macabre that surfaces throughout the book, with adjectives like "soot-streaked, simian, ghoulish . . . filled with the lust for destruction, he was like an imp from hell" (1941, 116). Clio's request for this level of annihilation fuels the demonic aspect of the resulting inferno, with something unwholesome about Clio's aspirations, from her blood obsession to the desire for unmaking she passes along to Cupide.

Once in Saratoga, however, the novel's mood switches to one befitting more lighthearted shenanigans than tearing a house down or sleeping in a bloodstained room as Clio, still using the guise of the Countess de Trenaunay de Chanfret, ensnares a rich man, a railroad magnate named Bart Van Steed. She and Clint pretend they have never met, and she remolds Saratoga society in a way only a Ferber heroine can. Among other trend-setting acts. including popularizing potato chips, Clio smokes in public and visits the male-dominated stables, a class and gender convention–flouting act that Lacey Lynnton also does in *Giant*. "Everything she did seemed unconventional because it was unexpected," Ferber writes. "The women found it most exasperating. The men found it piquant" (167). When Clint tells her that women don't visit the stables, she defies him. "'I'm going. I don't care what other women do. I'm different'" (179). And, in fact, her difference appears carnivalesque and even grotesque to the dowdies of Saratoga: Mrs. Van Steed, the rich mother of the man for whom Clio has set her cap, says, upon seeing her and her retinue, "What's this? We've not only a circus but a sideshow!" (224).

Clio, with her transgressive acts and defiant demeanor, stands in stark contrast to her rival for Van Steed's affections, the delicate Mrs. Porcelain, whose white eyelashes, the opposite of Clio's dark ones, Clio finds "annoying" (132). This difference, however, takes its toll. "Sometimes even she found it difficult to tell when she was herself and when she was the mysterious Mrs. De Chanfret. Perhaps no one enjoyed her performance more than she. Frequently she actually convinced herself of her own assumed role" (190). For all his stated complicity in Clio's plot to marry Van Steed, Clint resists her artifice as much as he can. He reads her "difference" as somehow emasculating to him, telling her, "'I reckon you'd best know that if you try to run me I'll leave you, pronto'" (177). Clio never pushes him enough to force him to make good on his threat, but when he accuses her of "play-acting," says, "'No. I am exactly what I said I would be when we planned it all in New Orleans. I did not pretend'" (209). Although her whole performance as the Countess is obviously "play-acting," Clio insists otherwise. With her convictions of her new role, and her ability to enjoy the performance, Clio carries on. Inasmuch as she wants to succeed in Saratoga's society, she remains true to herself, defying convention and relishing the resulting attention.

The matriarchal structure so often noted in Ferber's work becomes clear not only when Mrs. Van Steed's approval seems more important than that of her son, but also when local dowager Sophie Bellop, a rewritten Rachel Penny from *Come and Get It*, "adopts" Clio. She sees through Clio's sham title and praises her dramatic turns, but then tells her, "But from now on you'll need a strong arm behind you, and that handsome Texan's won't be enough. It's got to be a woman who's smarter than old lady Steed and who they're scared of" (227). Although it is a man whom Clio wishes to ensnare, it is the women around him—most importantly, his mother—who seem truly able to decide what will and will not happen. Clio attributes this to local class structure. "I suppose I was foolish to think that America was so simple. It's no good being grand and denying things and telling her to go" (227). Still, Clio does not capitulate. As un-"simple" as America proves to be, Clio continues to rely on herself and her servants to maintain her ever more plural identity. As she learns the complexities involved in American social climbing, Clio simply becomes more American by embracing them and standing firmly independent rather than relying on another person for help.

Bellop tells Clio that Mrs. Van Steed has been spreading rumors "'that you're an adventuress; that you've got a touch of the tarbrush!' Clio settled herself rather cozily as for a nap. 'There is much in what she says'" (250). There is no surprise or shame in people discovering the truth, Clio seems to say, only that their knowledge may alter the role she plays. If anything, she seems to grant a grudging respect to Mrs. Van Steed for knowing what is real. It causes her to revert to what she herself knows, and faced with Mrs. Bellop's information, Clio and Kaka form their own society of two. "There was something in her [Clio's] face and in the face of the Negress that made Sophie Bellop vaguely uncomfortable" (252), Ferber writes. Mrs. Bellop's unease may stem from her realization, initiated by Clio's admission of the "tarbrush" and furthered by a "they all look alike" kind of racist gaze, that both Clio and Kaka are African American.

Once Clio's "secret" is out to the matron, she embarks upon a plan that yields one of the most outlandish scenes in Ferber's novels, and one of the most exposed. This scene may have accounted for the classification

of the novel as stagey (although it was too intense for the film version of
the novel), but what may have originally been understood as theatrical
also can be read as a moment where the repressed—Clio's African American lineage—erupts when the clouding of her background proves too
onerous and simultaneously ridiculous.

The questions about Clio's race are on the minds of more Saratogans
than Mrs. Bellop, as the crowd assembled for the end-of-season ball murmurs, "'I always thought Creoles were colored people'" (270), furthering
the questions about Clio's background and the confusion over racially-
assigned nomenclature.[3] If she is a Creole, as the "murmurs" indicate,
then Creoles must be people of color, while Clio has tried to embrace her
Creole heritage as shorthand for European aristocracy. As the gathered
throngs expect Clio to appear as a French marquise, as she had told Sophie Bellop she would, Clio instead appears at the ball dressed as a New
Orleans praline vendor in over-the-top blackface:

> Praw-leens! Praw-leens! A clear powerful voice sounded from the
> outer corridor. In the doorway appeared a black mammy in volumi-
> nous calico and a vast white apron, a kerchief crossed on her bosom,
> her head swathed in a brilliant orange tignon. Gold and diamond hoop
> earrings dangled from beneath the turban's folds (Aunt Belle Piquery's
> jewelry). The teeth gleamed white in the blackened face, the dark eyes
> flashed, on her arm was a great woven basket neatly covered with a
> white napkin. The slim figure was stuffed fore and aft into ponderous
> curves. (274)

"'They'll never forgive,'" Mrs. Bellop says, but what won't "they" forgive
(274)? It is as if, after passing as the "Countesse de Choo Choo," as Bellop
calls her, for so long, Clio is turning the tables back on what can only be
called her audience. Having very nearly completed her pass—the "aristocratic" Van Steed asks for her hand to the ball, but she refuses him, preferring to wait for Clint—Clio attacks them by becoming the very thing

---

3. The word "Creole" has many differing definitions, but Clio claims her Creole father's
heritage as white European. See George Washington Cable's 1880 novel *The Grandissimes* for
a complex portrait of New Orleans society and its widely varying definitions of social groups.

they fear most. Instead of a white woman with "a touch of the tarbrush," Clio becomes the whole brush. She masks even her beauty, choosing to pad heavily the "slim figure" of which Ferber makes so much. "Don't," Bart Van Steed pleads, both seeming to entreat her to stop the spectacle and stop being a person of color and thus unfit to be his wife. She becomes a mammy, even after Kaka's protestations that she (Kaka) is no such thing, and wears the jewels of her prostitute aunt to heighten sexual connotation. She uses her polyglot abilities to speak in caricatured dialect, "'Go 'long, honey chile, you quality folks, you don't want no truck with a no-count black wench like me!'" (276).

The band strikes up a minstrel song, which she sings, and instead of shocked silence the gathered group begins singing along with Clio, despite the fact that "the faces of the satellite dowagers were masks of horror as they beheld the shuffling slapping feet, the heaving rump, the rolling eye, the insolent grin" (276). In her list of stereotypes and slurs, Ferber's narrative makes readers wonder what Clio's mask is—she is in disguise here, but her usual mask, of course, has its bizarre aspects as well, as Ferber makes clear—the clown-white face makeup is no less a mask than the praline-seller blackface. All can be regarded as "masks of horror," along with those of the Saratogans, both implicated in the performance and acting as its audience.

As Kaka, Sophie Bellop, and Clint all observe at different times, it is hard to know when Clio is playacting. Is the praline seller her real self, as she sees it? By unmasking the "darkest" secret she has, does Clio trump the ideas of herself as adventuress or whore, even more than being a bastard or the daughter of a prostitute? Is being black truly the most shocking thing to this assemblage? Eric Lott writes that minstrelsy includes "the dialectical flickering of racial insult and racial envy, moments of domination and moments of liberation, counterfeit and currency, a pattern at times amounting to no more than the two faces of racism, at others gesturing toward a specific kind of political or sexual danger, and all constituting a peculiarly American structure of racial feeling" (1995, 18). Clio's act, of course, is not that of an early blackface minstrel, but the elements Lott lists are in this complicated and multilayered scene. Clio uses the racial insults she has felt from questions about the "tarbrush," and her feeling that she is dominated by a society she wishes to ascend, to script her performance, which, for her, becomes a moment of liberation.

"By appearing as a caricature of what her audience believes her to be, she uncovers their unspeakable speculations on race and class and drags these ideas into public rather than private discourse," writes Campbell (2003, 37). With the performance aspect, however, the novel itself answers the question of the praline seller controlling this public space:

> She was Belle Piquery, she was Kakaracou and Cupide in the old carefree Southern days of her early childhood; she was defiance against every convention she so hated. And so shuffling, shouting, clapping her hands, the empty basket now hooked round her neck by its handle and hanging at her back, Clio Dulaine made her fantastic way to the veranda door that led onto the garden and disappeared from the sight of a somewhat hysterical company made up of the flower of Saratoga. (1941, 276)

Clio-as-praline-seller embodies people of different races who have all contributed to her identity. The Saratoga crowd has taken things away from her, symbolized by the empty praline basket, even as they thought she was the one scheming to pillage their society. The "somewhat hysterical" group shows them leaning toward her carnivalesque performance, enacting the age-old return of the repressed. At the same time, she performs as Lott's "currency," commodity, with the basket hung around her neck as if it were part of her body, the sweets available for the asking.

The masking and unmasking continue, just as Clio redecorated and then demolished her mother's Rampart Street house in New Orleans. Once Clio has left her audience, Kaka undoes the praline-seller costume, removing the dark makeup with cold cream. She is as "hysterical" as the abandoned ball-goers. She and Kaka reach a violent fever pitch at this upside-down moment, with Kaka accusing her of turning out just like her mother, being left by a man, as Clint has failed to appear at the ball. "With the flat of her hand Clio slapped the woman full in the face. But Kakacrou caught her hand and kissed it and said, 'Now! That is better. Now you will put on your pink satin and your mama's diamonds and Kaka fix your hair a la marquise'" (277). With her kiss, Kaka rejects the slap, a possible return for the one she gives Clio to undo her (Clio's) hysterics in New Orleans. She forces Clio to undo what she did with her praline-seller act. Now, Kaka decides, Clio will return as the whitest figure she can muster, demonstrating that she is actually a countess, not a slave. She will wear her mother's jewels as a symbol of "water-lily" purity instead of the baubles of a whore. Although she (Kaka) cannot cross back and forth over the color line with the fluidity of her mistress, she sees clearly where the power lies for Clio.

By redressing as the marquise, Clio undoes the transgression she has just performed. She seems to heed Bart's horrified "Don't," and Kaka's desire to clean the makeup off right away. At the same time, however, her ability to slide back and forth between mammy and marquise underlies her skill in molding society to her whim. In America, she can be whoever she likes. Clio heeds Kaka's desire to present her in her French finery. All Saratoga's attention is upon her when she reenters the ballroom, and when Clint returns, she chooses him for his vigor. It turns out that he has become a millionaire in the interim, so Clio receives the moneyed husband she has desired all along. All she says of her dramatic performance is: "The party seemed so dull and stuffy I thought I would liven it up a little. It was in fun" (279).

Clio's claim of "fun," juxtaposed with Ferber's use of "masks of horror," points toward the contradiction inherent in *Saratoga Trunk*. Clio's situation gives voice to some of Ferber's underlying questions and ideas about identity. "It was nowhere," she writes in "No Room at the Inn" of the place where the train carrying the Jews stops. "It was nothing. It was neither their country nor the adjoining country. It was no man's land" (1941, 17). The fate of the European Jews will not be shared in a country like America, where otherness and blended ethnicity are rewarded with success, Clio's story seems to announce, somewhat reassuringly. "No home, no name, no background, nothing," Clio says of herself in an echo of Ferber's phrasing in "No Room At the Inn." "I want comfort, security, money, respectability" (1941, 159). In America, so far from the ditch in which Niemand is born, Clio attains these sought-after things. *Saratoga Trunk* offers no easy answers: Clio gets where she wants by playacting, whether as a countess or as a grotesque parody of an African American praline vendor. Yet determination, the willingness to perform, passes all over the ethnic spectrum and the racial mixture that makes her hardly persevere until she receives her desired reward. The pat part of *Saratoga Trunk* is probably its Hollywood-ready ending, with marrying Clint as Clio's ultimate desire. Yet the rest of the novel demonstrates that nothing is easy about America's social and ethnic stratification, especially when various categories collide. Clio, however, prevails nonetheless. "I knew America would be like this, Clio Dulaine though, exultantly," Ferber writes. "Everything into the kettle, like a French pot-a-feu. Everything simmering together in a beautiful rich stew" (161).

7

BIG SPACES, BIG PROBLEMS
Giant

BESIDES *Show Boat,* THE 1952 NOVEL *Giant* is probably the most famous of Ferber's works, largely because of the James Dean and Elizabeth Taylor movie made from the novel. As one of her later and most noted works, *Giant* also takes an important place within the Ferber library. In *Giant,* Ferber explores the ways in which the dynastic nature of American families, at a personal and a societal level, both stymies and promotes their health, so that hybridization is not only a racial process but a cultural one as well. As a newly blended family—like *American Beauty*'s Orrange-Olzzaks, or *Come and Get It*'s Bostrom-Glasgows—faces the future, what happens? *Giant* pushes beyond questions of inter-white mixture to the notion of a society in which white and Mexican Americans join their families. In *Giant,* the process of becoming biracial is tested even further than in these other novels. The result is that, more directly than any of Ferber's other works, *Giant* tackles a larger and more fundamental question: who is an American?

With *Giant,* Ferber strives less to answer this question than to expose its many ramifications. She brings a young Virginian into the wide-open world of wealthy white Texans to gape along with her readers, but in the process of analyzing Texas, Leslie Lynnton becomes implicated in its complex and layered society as a Texan herself. *Giant* tackles regional boundaries within the United States as Leslie realizes the sharp differences between Virginia and Texas. More crucially, *Giant* delineates ethnic boundaries between white and Mexican Texans, but also draws sharply the class divisions that exist within these racial strata. As soon as one layer seems static, a new cast of characters appears to intersect and add another layer of meaning and interdependence. The poor white farm-hand's struggle is contrasted with that of the poverty-stricken Mexican Americans who work on the same ranch, and Leslie's attempt to make sense of the rigid cultural mores evolves into a complex blend of indebt-edness and noblesse oblige.

Giant has incurred more criticism—and ire—over the years than many of Ferber's other works. Jonathan Yardley wrote in a 2006 *Washington Post* column in which he revisits classic novels that "Reading *Giant* for a second time was a painful, if not outright excruciating, experience. What was received half a century ago as a withering satire of Texas nouveau riche now has all the subtlety of a bludgeon. Aspiring to irony, Ferber rarely rises above sarcasm. Her prose is almost entirely lacking in grace or rhythm" (2006, C1). Yardley goes on to praise the film version while continuing to excoriate the novel: "I could go on and on about the ways in which the movie improves upon the book—it's tighter, more smoothly paced, funnier, more dramatic—but few people who know both are likely to disagree" (C2). This stance misses some of the most compelling parts of *Giant,* which are the points of pressure Ferber places upon the ques-tions of race in Texas. Also, anyone opening a Ferber book is presumably not looking for subtlety or tightness. The movie may be livelier, funnier, and even easier to swallow, but *Giant* is still worth the read.

Yet Yardley is hardly *Giant's* sole critic, nor is he the only person to find the book worthy of scrutiny. The topic of *Giant* even came up during the McCarthy hearings, as Ann Shapiro points out. The novel had been reviewed on Voice of America radio, bringing it to Senator Joseph McCar-thy's attention. At a hearing, he rhetorically asked a Voice of America em-ployee: "If I were a member of the Communist Party, and I wanted to dis-credit America and further the Communist cause, could you think of any better job I could do helping out the Communist cause than by beaming to Europe the type of material which you have just described?" (Shapiro 2008, 18). To critics like McCarthy, Ferber's Texas was un-American, and along with the senator from Wisconsin, Texans hated the novel. In her second autobiography, *A Kind of Magic,* Ferber writes that Texas headlines said, "We think she ought to be caught and hanged here in Texas and we'll arrange the hanging and choose the people to hold the rope" (1963,

197). Meanwhile, Ferber felt that she had, if anything, underplayed Texas: "I had, in fact, felt it necessary to play down or even to eliminate some of the facts and situations and behaviorisms encountered in the violent mores of this unique society" (197). She plaintively adds that she told those she met in Texas that she was visiting as a writer, but no one understood that meant she would use anecdotes she experienced in the book.

So once the book came out, Texans rebelled. "As has been noted through vibrations felt easily from Houston to New York, a fair share of Texas has failed to find in *Giant* the substance for amusement. Large chunks of a large state are mad in a large way," wrote Lewis Nichols in the *New York Times Book Review* (1952, 30). And not even everyone in New York liked it. "There is a tone to the book that is more reproving than reportorial. It is some fine writing by Edna Ferber. But it is not fine Edna Ferber. . . . Not by a long shot, pardner!" wrote William Juengst in the *Brooklyn Eagle* (1952). As Oklahomans were with *Cimarron*—and eventually, Oklahomans invited Ferber to take part in a dedication of a Pioneer Woman statue—Texans were not to be mollified until the story returned, re-formed with Hollywood glamour.

As Shapiro writes, *Giant* was Ferber's first novel written after World War II. "When the war was over, Ferber seems to have become obsessed once more with the plight of people who, like Jews, were persecuted because of their ethnicity. The result was *Giant*" (2008, 20). The Mexicans—or "Mexican-Americans," as Ferber, an early hyphenator, often calls them—do retain some "Jewish" qualities, particularly when described as representative of "ancient" cultures, recalling the ways in which Ferber characters like Sol Levy and Clarence Heyl explain their Jewishness. In *Giant,* Ferber consistently reminds readers of the cultural debt owed Mexico by Texans, and complicates depictions with a similarly acute awareness of cultural appropriation. "[E]very American cowboy all the way from Montana down to Arizona and Texas had copied from the Mexican" (1952, 119). With images of masks, copying, and costumes, Ferber describes a society rife with slippage between authenticity and show. Without depending upon a literal performance framework like the one in *Show Boat, Giant* nevertheless raises similar questions of ownership and domain.

Giant approaches these ethnic concerns through the vector of a large Texas cattle-ranching family named Benedict, plunged into change when

Bick Benedict marries Leslie Lynnton. Instead of trying to force her new home to resemble her old one, as Sabra Cravat does in *Cimarron*, Leslie demands that her new home change. From the outset, Leslie takes on Texas society, most notably attacking the local Anglo tradition of mistreating Mexican Americans. In a line echoing the opening of *Gone With The Wind*—"Scarlett O'Hara was not beautiful, but men seldom realized it when caught by her charm as the Tarleton twins were" (Mitchell 1936, 1)—Ferber writes, "Though the three Lynnton girls always were spoken of as the Beautiful Lynnton Sisters of Virginia they weren't really beautiful" (1952, 65). Even before Leslie arrives in Texas, she is well accustomed to servants who are people of color. In Virginia, history-reading and often righteous Leslie makes a salvo, telling Bick she's learned that "we" stole Texas from the Mexicans. Leslie's southernness is complicated by having been born in Ohio—as she claims, "'I'm not a Virginian'" (92). Her father, Race Lynnton, agrees: "'You'd have been good in the Civil War, hiding slaves in the Underground'" (92). These early details position Leslie as inherently conflicted, a freedom fighter dwelling in a house relying upon the consistent pampering of "colored" servants (80).

Race also introduces Bick to "the young Negro who drove them. . . . The little ceremony was as casual (but also as formal) as though he were introducing any two friends or acquaintances. 'Benedict, this is Jefferson Swazey who'll drive us down. Jeff, this is Mr. Jordan Benedict from Texas.' 'Well I'll be damned,' thought Jordan Benedict" (71). While Ferber couches this ritual as similar to one between equals, and Bick's astonishment reveals his belief that Race acts with unbecoming egalitarianism, Bick is still introduced as "Mr.," while Jefferson Swazey is "Jeff." These are not actually equals. The African American driver bears the name of probably American history's most noted Virginian slaveholder, the man who wrote, "I tremble for my country when I reflect that God is just." The question of the servant class, particularly as it involves racial and ethnic stratification, suffuses *Giant* as the novel's plot heads west. Bick's repulsion at his host's informality serves to underscore the ways in which hegemonically framed societies propagate their old ways.

Ferber relies upon the connection between the Old South and the Old West to push the novel's tensions into production. In Texas, Leslie sees that "[t]he dark faces of the station loungers were unlike the submissive masks of Negroes she knew so well in Virginia. . . . Nothing followed the look or pattern of the life she had left behind her" (109). Leslie has internalized the idea of submission as a mask. She instantly compares the Mexican Americans at the station with African Americans at home, just as she notes that the cabins she sees in Texas are "'flimsier, even, than the Negro cabins she had seen so familiarly in Virginia'" (157) and that "'the vaquero's horrible little shacks were worse than the Negro cabins in my Virginia'" (434).

The Benedicts maintain a "Big House," a "pseudo-Spanish palace of stone and concrete and iron that was foreign to the Texas land and had been rejected by it" (128). With this image, Ferber initiates a metaphor for the Texas of *Giant*. The members of the Anglo ruling class are all "pseudo-Spanish," in the sense of pretending aristocracy. Leslie imagines that Bick's sister Luz "was acting a part. Was purposely talking a kind of native lingo" (131). The Benedicts in Texas fulfill a self-assigned role, maintaining the local hierarchy with their combination of folksy diction and hegemonic behavior. Although Leslie is typically the more introspective member of the couple, Bick also reveals that he contemplates their life and its reliance upon old ethnic hierarchies: "'This is the real Spanish-Mexican barbecue. . . . They despise what we Americans call a barbecue—meat roasted over coals. This pit cooking is the real Mexican barbacoa. That's where we get the word" (177). Bick's summary of the local cuisine evinces a nuanced understanding of the dish's culinary history, but also demonstrates his comprehension of the anxiety surrounding the Texas social order. Dividing the Mexican Americans from "we Americans," and reporting their distaste for the bastardized "barbecue," Bick identifies some salient sites of anxiety. This vividly authentic presentation, however, physically affects Leslie, who faints at the sight of some Mexican cooks wiping calves' brains from inside the skull with bread. Even with her respect for the non-appropriated dish, Leslie literally cannot stomach something so "real."

Leslie's own concept of America includes "awfully American things. Like pork and beans. And Fourth of July. And Vermont. And pumpkin pie. And Fords. And Sunday school. And in Ohio, when I was a child" (202). With this roster, she assembles a list of items that contradict those found in the America of Texas. Prosaic, homely food like pork and beans and the traditional Thanksgiving pumpkin pie seem unavailable in the Texan menu of "barbacoa." The cool green state of Vermont has as little to do with Texas's landscape as the "cocky Midwestern hired girls" do with the often beleaguered Mexican American servants in Benedict. When Bick tells Leslie that one of his vaqueros always sleeps outside his door, she exclaims: "It's feudal! It's uncivil—" (202). Although frequent parallels are drawn between the Mexican Americans in Texas and the African Americans in Virginia, Leslie's introduction of the Ohio hired girl demonstrates her vision of a servant who works but is simultaneously "cocky," suggesting potential defiance but also life and energy even when performing menial tasks. As she tells Bick: "'I've been here two days and every natural thing I've said and done has been forbidden. . . . Speaking to the employees as if they were human beings like myself" (197). Clearly, Leslie's father's addressing his driver as "Jeff" and introducing him to Bick forms her comprehension of equal treatment, so that the Virginia household's own failings fade in comparison to the overt discrimination she sees in Texas.

The matter of servant and master relations pervades the novel, with Bick and Leslie believing they are on opposing sides. "'I'm not Simon Legree, you know,'" Bick says, in a direct fling at Leslie's Virginia (209). Actually, there are some similarities between Bick and Legree, the notoriously evil slave-owner in Harriet Beecher Stowe's *Uncle Tom's Cabin*, published one hundred years earlier than *Giant*. While the Benedict employees are not slaves, they are nevertheless imprisoned by a toxic cycle of poverty, ill health, and feudalistic attitudes. If Leslie is obsessed with the poor quality of life that many Mexican Americans have, Bick is conscious of it as well, and arms himself with southern history as his defense. When Leslie mentions the Mexican workers' "shanties," he says, "'I noticed your nigger cabins in the dear old South weren't so sumptuous'" (259). Leslie reads from a Texas guidebook that says that Mexican workers earn $1.56 a week, and Bick asks, "'How would you have liked it if I'd told you how Virginia—'" (287). Leslie tells Bick that he unfairly uses the Mexican vote in the small town of Benedict, and his retort is "'Uh-huh. Like your Negro vote in the South'" (324).

This syllogism of Leslie as the southern belle is fraught due to her Ohio origins, which ally her more with the "cocky" hired girls and pumpkin pie she remembers from her brief but evidently formative Ohio years. Even Bick often calls Leslie a "Yankee" (324, 325, 334), creating a dichotomy that leaves him as purely Texan—its own idiosyncratic identity— while Leslie—her father's Underground Railroad worker—personifies the North despite her Virginia home. Leslie's ability to embody more than one label, however, demonstrates part of what she sees lacking in her adopted state. As she tells Bick, "'You're still fighting Mexicans and Indians and orange soufflés. Give up. Adapt yourselves. They're here to stay'" (265). Leslie acknowledges the inevitability of change, but is also confronted with the stratifications of the societies-within-societies that make up Texas at mid-century and that confuse her as she navigates the apartheid of her adopted home, and imagines white Texans' forbears coming in a surge from the North:

> Arrogantly, in defiance of their Mexican compatriots, they wore Northern clothes, these good solid citizens. . . . "We're the white Americans, we're the big men, we eat the beef and drink the bourbon, we don't take siestas, we don't feel the sun, the heat or the cold, the wind or the rain, we're Texans. So they drank gallons of coffee and stayed awake while the Mexican Americans quietly rested in the shade, their hats pulled down over their eyes; and the Negroes vanished from the streets." (224)

Ferber takes pains to employ a conjoined ethnonym—"Mexican Americans" —to describe those already in Texas, a calculated phrase considering the consistent divisions between "Mexicans" and "Americans" throughout *Giant*. With the contrast between wakeful northern aggressors and somnolent people of color, Ferber imagines a Texas plundered by the very people—the Benedicts and their ilk—who now claim the term "Texan" for themselves.

When Luz dies, Benedicts arrive from "Antoine's in New Orleans, from their suites at the Mark Hopkins in San Francisco, from their tennis in Long Island, from the golf links of White Sulphur" (235). The far-flung Benedicts represent a pampered leisure class supported by the cattle ranch of Texas, which has the simultaneous effect of making the wealthy Bick seem like a dutiful farm manager and implicating the whole country's well-heeled in Texas's racial divide. Leslie dubs one of the relatives,

Uncle Bawley Benedict, "refreshing" because he says that Texans are "acting all the time, most of them. Playing Texas" (243), evoking the earlier image of Anglo Texans taking on some of the customs of the vanquished as well as Luz's affected folksiness. Bawley assesses the local language and hybridized culture as "'a mixture of Spanish and Mexican and Nigrahs and French and German and folks from all over the whole country. It settled into a kind of jargon, but we play it up'" (245). The idea of "playing it up" heightens the image of Texas as performance, a play with specific costumes and its own script, while the polyglot lingo—again, with the implication of people from "all over the whole country" involved—portrays a region produced by mixture. As with Ferber's books that more self-consciously include performative aspects—the medicine show in *American Beauty,* the ball in *Saratoga Trunk,* the plays in *Show Boat*—race becomes the ultimate thematic concern, less easily donned and doffed than costumes and dialect.

Leslie explores the poorer sections of Benedict—where she finds and nurses an ill mother and child—as well as a migrant laborer camp. Opening a shack door, a pregnant Leslie finds another sick woman inside. This time, however, the patient is not Mexican: "'I am American,' the girl said. Now Leslie, accustomed to the half-light of the tent, saw that the pinched and grayish face was that of a girl not more than seventeen. She felt her own face flaming scarlet. There! she said to herself. Take that!" (276). Peering behind the curtain established by her husband's Texan mores reveals to Leslie a reflection of herself: a white woman, recently pregnant, just like Leslie. The event destroys Leslie's primary assumption about the camp and its laborers—that they are places for Mexican people—at the same time that it reinforces her vision of them as unsanitary and desperate places. Leslie finds herself so undone that she thrusts whatever cash she has at the young woman, demonstrating that all that separates them is money. She can no longer pretend that Bick, easily cast as the Simon Legree of the situation, is keeping only Mexicans in such a deprived state. Here she finds an "American"—white—woman, a reflection of her own societal status, in as dire a situation as the Mexican laborers she predicted would be there.

Leslie sees not only Texas's present as flawed, but its past as well. Studying the art displayed at the Alamo, Leslie sees that "[i]nvariably there were the brave white Americans rising superior over the dark-skinned Mexicans" (291). "And which was right and which was wrong? Leslie asked herself. And which was aggressor and which defender?" (291). Leslie's ability to step back from the societal imperative dictating that the white settlers defending the Alamo were in the right gives her a doubled identity as an adoptive Texan. Concurrent with this exposure, she meets sympathetic native Texans like Uncle Bawley, who says, "you might say the whole of Texas was built . . . on the bent backs of Mexicans. Don't let on to Bick I said that'" (320). Bawley understands the flaws of his hegemonic society and even comprehends whose work established the Texas he loves. Yet he also wishes to hide that understanding, especially from Bick, who represents the racist system.

For all her enunciated sympathy, however, Leslie is not consistently sensitive. When she feels unattractive, she says, "'I feel like a squaw'" (331). In the water town of Vientecito for a celebration called Fiesta, a fellow guest says to Leslie, "'You'd never believe you were in the United States, would you?' 'Never,' Leslie said. 'Never'" (337). She seems to comprehend inequality relentlessly, but labors to understand the complexities of heterogenous cultures blending, such as in the example of the Americans of Vienticito. One way Ferber delves into this thorny territory is to set Texas in contrast with other societies, including other American regions. Returning to Virginia for a visit, Leslie hangs around the family cook, a "gifted woman" named Caroline (345). Leslie asks for recipes, but Caroline tells her, "A body cain't be so businessified about how much this and how much that, Miss Leslie. I just th'ow in'" (345). She is not wanted in the kitchen. Also, Leslie is not learning these recipes to cook herself, but to teach to her Mexican cook, who is not "very gifted with our kind of cooking" (345). Caroline, who speaks with Ferber's version of a southern African American dialect, is positioned as "our kind" of servant—familiar to Leslie and able to provide appropriate food in contrast with the non-"gifted" Mexican cook in Texas. Although she fights for the rights of the downtrodden at home, some of Bick's southern-belle criticisms seem apt when read alongside the image of Leslie in the kitchen, pleading with the family retainer for recipes from home.

Visiting Texas on an extended family vacation, Leslie's father, upon whom she has patterned her social awareness, says, "This is a civilization psychologically. . . . The South is a problem, certainly; and the Eastern

seaboard. . . . But this!'" (358). Texas defies definition even for this self-professedly liberal thinker. Her brother-in-law casts the Mexicans as "a problem," prompting Race to retort: "imagine the problem we were to them when we came swarming in a hundred years ago. We were the foreigners then'" (358). Race's comment emphasizes the slippage between "we" and "foreigners," highlighting the shift in power in Texas's history that has taken the Mexican residents from "we" to "foreigner" in a matter of years. For Ferber, the question of whether Texas can retain any of the moral high ground when confronted with these challenges rests on the white Texans' treatment of the Mexicans and Mexican Americans who live near them and work for them.

These tensions combine in one anecdote that throws into relief the extent of ethnic boundaries and cultural differences that bind Texas. Leslie explains to houseguests that her son's playmate, Angel, is a boy despite his dress and long curls. His parents, believing childlessness was a punishment for desiring only a boy, had promised God that if they were given a child, they would carefully tend his or her hair until it was a foot long, and then "it will be cut off by the priest and placed as an offering on the shrine" (363). The reactions to Angel's story range from horror to fascination:

> "Barbaric!" said Lady Karfrey.
> "By that time," Doctor Horace mused, "he'll be so confused as to be incoherent. Or such a tough guy, in self-defense, that Reata Ranch can't hold him." . . .
> "Do you think," Nancy Lynnton demanded, "that this child is a fit playmate for Jordy!" (363)

The crossing of a gender boundary strikes many of the family members as elementally problematic, exposing anxieties about the seemingly disparate cultures housed within Texas society. The way in which Angel's situation is described—offerings placed, a priest, a punitive God—is read as outlandish by the Lynntons. Yet Bick, typically presented as the chauvinistic Anglo Texan, admires Angel, even comparing him favorably with his own son: "'This kid is a tough hombre. In fact, I wish Jordy had some of his stuff'" (363). Bick is more comfortable with the rituals associated with Angel than with the view of his female garb as "barbaric" or "unfit," demonstrating his increased comfort with Mexican American culture rather than the kind of "American" society represented by Leslie's family. A cross-dressing boy is more manly, in Bick's eyes, than his own son. Race's final take on Angel—and Texas—is: "'This could be wonderful. . . . Maybe someday it will be'" (363). Yet Ferber leaves unclear the process of how Angel's cross-dressing will go from being read as barbaric to wonderful.

Bick's prediction proves accurate in some ways: "Of the two inevitable reactions to his childhood years of petticoat servitude he had chosen the tough one. . . . He and his friend affected a bastard dialect made up of Mexican jargon, American slang, Spanish patois. . . . The Reata vaqueros said of him, in Spanish, 'He's trying to change the color of his eyes to blue'" (385). Angel, so long dressed across gender, begins to privilege his American—in this case, Anglo—interests, a tendency deemed every bit as "barbaric" to his own family as his upbringing in dresses was to Jordy's family. In "trying to change the color of his eyes," Angel's language choices evolve. With his hybrid way of speaking, Angel is viewed as rejecting his own background even as he struggles to enunciate it in his own way.

His Benedict counterpart faces the same charges, but for very different reasons. When Bick sees Jordy sit next to a Mexican American girl named Juana, Bick bristles and Leslie scolds him not to be "feudal" (414). It turns out, however, that Juana and Jordy are secretly married. Jordy vows to become a doctor and treat Mexican American patients. "'You're all alike, you kids today, white and Mexican, you and Angel Obregon. No damn good,'" Bick rails (408). While the hybrid future that Jordy and Juana's children will carve for Texas demonstrates forward-thinking change, Bick cannot see past his prejudices, leaving him to voice disappointment both in his son and in Angel, whose Mexican American culture he has so recently defended.

Despite Bick's changed opinion, Angel proves his American-ness when he dies in World War II. Ferber's description of treatment of the Mexican American war dead illustrates the multiple forces at work in Texas race relations:

> the undertaker in Benedict—Funeral Director he now was called—
> said that naturally he could not handle the funeral of a Mexican.

Old Angel, a man of spirit, said that his son was an American; and that there had been Mexicans in Texas when Christopher Columbus landed on the continent of North America. But the Funeral Director— Waldo Shute his name was—big fellow—said Angel should take the box to Nopal, why not? Someone—there were people who said it might have been Leslie Benedict—thought this was not quite right. Talk got around, it reached a busy man who was president of the United States of America way up north in Washington, D.C. So he had the flag-draped box, weary now of its travels, brought to Washington and buried in the cemetery reserved for great heroes, at Arlington. Marita wished that it could have been nearer Benedict, so that she might visit her husband's grave. But she was content, really. (415)

As she does throughout the novel, Leslie crosses cultural boundaries to perform what she deems a righteous and just act, defying the bigoted funeral director and defending the older Angel, who uses Ferber's line of argument originally associated with Jews—the age of a culture—to demonstrate his entitlement to all the respect America has to offer. The invocation of the president validates Leslie's actions and serves as a rebuke to Waldo Shute, the "big fellow" who embodies the stereotype of the oversized white Texan. Yet Leslie's mission to have Angel buried in Arlington seems vexed, with his wife's inability to visit his grave. Ferber employs a circumspect telling to give the story a feeling of hearsay, as it might have been passed around in the Benedict community. The tone of questionable veracity overlaying each segment underscores the instability of the ethnic classification at play.

Jordy's wife Juana, who "moved and spoke in the manner of an ancient people in an ancient land" (26), adds to the elder Angel Obregon's evocation of the venerable age of her culture, appending Mexican Americans to the ethnicities that, like Jewish people in the tradition of orientalism, represent gravity because of their culture's age. Mingling their heritages, Jordy and Juana name their son Polo, but call him Jordan. The child has "the café-au-lait coloring of his Mexican grandmother and great-grandmother" (432), and much of the rest of the novel forces the issue of Texas ethnicity in a time in which Benedict is no longer a purely Anglo name. When Bick brags about Jordan's horseback-riding ability (as he did Angel's), his friend Pinky says, "'Well, real Mexican—'" (419), but stops himself. The rest of the sentence would have cast Bick's grandson in a stereotype of what "real Mexicans" do—in this formulation, they are talented riders as young children—in a way that demonstrates how fundamental a shift Bick's family undergoes. At a party, Pinky's wife Vashti makes a similar slip when she asks Juana why she wears black "'Like a Mex—'" because she cannot believe she is speaking to a Mexican at a social event (27).

This change is emblematized when Leslie, her daughter Luz, Juana, and the child Jordy stop in a café along a road at which the owner tells them, "'We don't serve Mexicans here'" (438). Luz shouts "'I'll tell my father! He'll kill you!'" (439), but Leslie prevents her from giving his name. Patriarchy reigns: although Bick never hides his feelings about race mixing, Luz believes that his name wields enough power to solve her problems. The specter of passing is also raised. As they hurry out, the waitress says, "'You crazy, Floyd! Only the kid and his ma was cholos, not the others!'" "'Aw, the old one was, black hair and sallow, you can't fool me,'" he responds (439–40).

In this episode, Leslie blends into the people with whom she claims sympathy. Her dark coloring means her appearance, depending upon her company, can either identify her as the white Leslie Lynnton Benedict or as a Mexican grandmother. Removed from her typically high social context in a roadside diner, Leslie is subject to the same treatment as her Mexican American relatives:

> Quietly Leslie said, "We're furious because of what that ignorant bigot did. But we all know this has been going on for years and years. It's always happened to other people. Now, it's happened to us. The Benedicts of Reata. So we're screaming." . . . And deep inside her a taunting voice said, Oh, so now you're doing it too, h'm? After twenty-five years of nagging and preaching and being so superior you're evading too. Infected. (442)

Leslie now sees the act of being a racist white Texan as a disease with which one becomes "infected," much like the physical illnesses Jordy and

Juana fight in the vaqueros' village. With the same incident, she becomes both victim—of the bigot's discriminatory ire—and bystander to oppression, with her knowledge that such incidents have been "going on for years and years."

Leslie serves as a vector for bringing both self-knowledge and a mixed family to Bick, and does not shrink from chastising, telling him that "doing things against your feelings and principles" over the years has harmed him (445). Countering her slightly patronizing candor—and her possibly over-generous faith in his "principles"—Bick allows his racist vitriol and conflicted beliefs to flow as when he considers his son's choices: "'Down in Spigtown with the greasers in Vientecito, a shingle on the door right along with a fellow named Guerra. . . . Juana and the kids . . . Juana's all right she's a decent girl she's Jordy's wife Jordy Benedict's wife and the kid looks like a real cholo'" (446). In this rant, a more articulate follow-up to the racist speech Elly gives Julie in *Show Boat*—Bick musters all the anti-Mexican slurs he can—"greasers," "Spigtown," "cholo"—to express his disbelief and disappointment at his new merged family. Interspersed with this are his slightly positive comments about Juana, but the overriding retention of racial insults demonstrates the lengths to which Bick's understanding of the Mexican people he has always lived with is framed by derogatory assumptions.

This anticlimactic interchange concludes *Giant,* leaving open the conflict over the vast and contested Texas. The new generation of Benedicts are profitably blended with the Mexican American culture, achieving a positively charged future in an ethnically mixed—and by now, classically Ferber—landscape. By exposing Bick's prejudices and Leslie's vexed and double-conscious examination of their shared society, the novel concludes with less of a finale than with a re-opening of earlier themes with an added understanding of the way in which individuals inherit and affect their own societies. Earlier novels like *Cimarron* and *American Beauty* conclude with turbulence, preoccupied with the ways in which individuals craft their identities, clamoring for their own reasons to call themselves Americans. In the end of *Giant,* the enormousness of the challenge grows overwhelming, even as characters continue to search for these sometime esoteric self and group definitions. Only a character like Leslie, a peripatetic bystander, who internalizes the turmoil and struggle as well as participating in it, can attempt to explain to her distraught husband: "'It's a thousand other things. Oil. And the ranch. And the Mexicans. The bigotry. The things that can happen to decent people. It's going to catch up with you. With everybody. It always does'" (446).

Conclusion

THE GREAT WHITE NORTH
Great Son and *Ice Palace*

BOOKENDING *Giant* CHRONOLOGICALLY, the 1945 novel *Great Son* and the 1948 *Ice Palace* share the well-worn Ferber themes of race and class in America. Both works, however, deal with a wider range of ethnicities than *Giant,* and return to the hectic recitations of Swede-Basque-Jewish-Dutch people of the earlier novels. Also, both evince a concern with northern American regions. These two works, on Seattle and Alaska, concern societies working to amalgamate sharply different communities into cohesive groups while maintaining sufficient recognition of ethnic identities to keep them alive and relevant. In other words, both *Great Son* and *Ice Palace* fulfill Ferber's career-long comprehension of the intricate and sometimes volatile ways in which each of John Dewey's hyphens "connects instead of separates" (1916, 127).

As Ferber's previous novels demonstrate, preparing for the American future involves an understanding of the inevitability of blending identities, as well as comprehension of Ferber's tensions inherent within such hybridization. Both of these novels expand upon her characteristic focus on the life-giving process of ethnic mixing, and the idea that Americans continually improve with each generation as they meld and diversify. With their explosion of ethnic identities—and between just these two books, Ferber writes about people defined by words including "Indian," "Chinese," "Jewish," "Japanese," "Eskimo," "French," and "Scotch"—the texts bring to a head the robust confusion and cacophony of ethnicities proliferating as fast as the country's population and racial self-consciousness.

Throughout her work, Ferber makes clear that these ethnic considerations are minefields that are nevertheless worthy of exploration by reader, characters, and author. The racist language of some of her earlier novels exposes the social unease of America at large. From the murder of Isaiah in *Cimarron* to the downfall of Julie in *Show Boat* to the unsung war death of Angel in *Giant,* Ferber's characters fall prey to the debilitating effects of America's ethnic stratification. Similar crises frame *Great Son* and *Ice Palace,* but both books resolutely represent their American moments as times of great potential. In these two forward-looking books, the joy inherent in Clarence Heyl's inspirational lecture in *Fanny Herself* seems possible again. *Great Son* and *Ice Palace* convey Ferber's undimmed resolve to portray the unrelentingly complicated future of America as a fraught, but nevertheless spectacular, prospect.

The time in which *Great Son* and *Ice Palace* were written offered its own challenges, which Ferber tackled personally as well as on paper. In 1944, she met with *New York Times* publisher Arthur Sulzberger. "Wanted to talk with him about the critical Anti-Semitic condition growing here," she wrote, "but he babbled on and on about himself and it all came to nothing" (qtd. in Gilbert 1978, 266). Ferber's riposte is designed to cover her intense concern about a serious problem. In writing these two novels, she would find more ways to confront her anxiety over the war and the way in which it highlighted both ethnic differences and how these differences were treated. Her talk with Sulzberger may have come to a frustrating "nothing," but Ferber's own literary production framed her distress in a way that attempted to make sense of America's pivotal role in an uneasy moment.

In *Great Son,* Ferber traverses themes of classification and ethnic hegemony, including the very anti-Semitism about which she strove to warn Sulzberger. The novel, which foreshadows the concern with Alaska that would become *Ice Palace,* centers on a large westering family named Melendy. Dancer Pansy DeLeath bears Vaughan Melendy's child in the Alaskan gold mines, and then Vaughan and his wife adopt the boy Dike, creating a charged family situation that sets off the dynastic tensions that motivate the novel. "The success of Great Son is assured," said an article in *Time* magazine. "The Literary Guild alone is printing 450,000 copies, Cosmopolitan has serialized it, and Broadway Producer Mike

Todd has reputedly paid $200,000 for the movie rights" ("Ferber Fundamentals," 1945). Audiences were rapacious for a new Ferber saga. In some ways, however, *Great Son* revisited an old one, since it functions in some ways as a remapping of the 1935 *Come and Get It*. Vaughan Melendy, "Seattle's millionaire lumber baron and salmon king" (1945, 86) is a "benevolent giant"—nicknamed "Tikkum," just as *Come and Get It*'s Barney is "Gusto" (and Jordan Benedict becomes "Bick.") His dour patrician wife is named Emmy, similar in name and personality to Emma Louise, Barney Glasgow's wife. Ferber even recycles the surname Melendy, evocative of the Tom Melendy family of Wisconsin in the earlier novel. Pansy De-Leath's dark eyes and dance hall–girl profession call to mind Lotta Morgan's. Furthering the play on characters' nomenclature is that the names are combined in an actual woman named Vaughan De Leath, a famous woman crooner of the 1920s. (She sang "Are You Lonesome Tonight?" in 1927, long before Elvis Presley recorded it.)

Great Son leaves the dance hall for graver subjects and a more prescient historical era, however. Set against the backdrop of the events leading up to World War II, the novel's action occurs in Seattle just before Pearl Harbor. The characters include ethnically charged individuals such as a Jewish refugee and a Japanese American family, who illustrate the intricacies of and tensions within a striated America on the brink of war. *Great Son* begins, atypically, with a weary-sounding apologia. Ferber writes, "Back and forth, in and out, weave the people in this book. . . . This, then, is not so much a novel as a character outline of what will, someday, at other hands, be a stupendous and dazzling piece of Americana" (8). *Great Son* is indeed one of Ferber's least famous novels, perhaps because of its fairly—if self-consciously—diffident structure, starting with this out-of-character acknowledgement that others might carry her own themes further. Reviewers tended to agree with Ferber's contrite introduction: "In this clear criticism of the exploitative philosophy of life, Miss Ferber's well-written and entertaining novel has more value than in its bizarre and somewhat artificial people and plot" (Frederick 1945, 35). Now as then, *Great Son* itself functions as a rich "piece of Americana" with its contextualized rumination on the importance of race and identity within a national framework, set as it is against the heightened realities of a multiply ethnic nation at a crossroads.

Vaughan's dynasty, and the self-referential American journey, begins with Exact Melendy, his nonagenarian and lifelong Seattle resident mother, a woman who would have seemed at home in *American Beauty*'s New England with her Mayflower-inflected name. Her primogeniture actually stems, however, from her status as an early West Coast settler to Washington state. As the family discusses the encroaching conflict, Exact argues for exclusion while her grandson Mike objects:

> "What's it our business? Same way with the Civil War. I recollect Pa said keep out of it let the North and South scrap it out, none of the Northwest's business, he said. Slaves. What's slavery got to do with us, he said."
>
> "So," Mike drawled, "we imported a lot of Japs and Chinese, and if you think that isn't going to be something someday."
>
> Sharply Vaughan demanded, "What makes you say that? Crazy thing like that?" (68)

The family splits along generational lines only with Dike's son Mike, who counts Japanese Americans as his friends and seems to comprehend the result of years of anti-Asian discrimination. Exact, meanwhile, finds the concept of isolationism appropriate even when it seemed impossible given that the war in question—the Civil War—involved her own country. Her sympathy with her father's question—"What's slavery got to do with us"—demonstrates an even more provincial worldview, in which living in the western portion of the country excuses an American from caring about the war based in its eastern part. Mike, as the American future, possesses hope for an understanding of the transferability of bigotry, and the danger of any hegemonic culture, while his grandfather's horrified anecdotal response reveals his anxiety regarding his own place in that culture. The overlapping commentary serves to emphasize the clannish nature of white Americans while emphasizing the dramatic shift in outlook, from Exact's appalled isolationism to Mike's expansive view. In the middle, Vaughan enunciates his stance: "'The Melendys are good, solid American citizens and have been for I don't know how long—oldest settlers and you know it'" (88). His identity intertwines with his family's protracted legacy as "Americans," so that his own authenticity prevails above all. His comment comes across as a studied attempt to launch the argument that he is owed any social ease he enjoys, while his son Mike recognizes the tensions with which that entitled view is fraught. As the steward of the future, Mike sees a world alive with Ferber's ethnic mixtures, which is going to "be something someday," a phrase implying that the status quo is unsatisfactory.

Like Mike, Pansy is more amenable to a vision of American heterogeneity. She situates herself as a healthy blend. As she says, "Ma was a mixture of Irish and French and American and Scotch thrown in, and the Scotch never had a chance" (54). This contrasts with Emmy's maternal claim that her mother "was old New England stock and she brought me up just so" (54). With Emmy's repressed ways, the New England lineage she evokes is clearly the pinched place of the rotten-at-the-core aunts of *So Big* and the macabre society of *American Beauty*, both doomed in contrast to sites more nurturing to "mixtures" (albeit all-white) such as Pansy. Just as Selina stays out west to avoid her bitter aunts, and the Polish immigrants overturn the gothic, diseased Connecticut, the New England to which *Great Son* refers forms a place to strive against. With Mike's capable attitude, the Pacific Northwest belongs to the forward-looking, not those mired in the American past.

In contrast to the self-important but similarly aged Vaughan, Pansy understands groups other than those forming her own background. "Life was kaleidoscopic" for the young Pansy, and direct images of shifting colors and patterns pervade the text. The Chinese people she sees as a young girl are "strange yellow men [who] had built the railroads of the West . . . civilization itself had benefited enormously from the presence of these Orientals in the New World. Seattle had driven them out barbarously" (103). Although she refers to them as "strange" and "yellow," Ferber's understanding of the Chinese laborers' contribution as well as her use of the term Oriental—her term, of course, for wise, sensitive Jews—forms an argument for the advantages of a society based upon multiple participants. Ferber's comprehension of the damage ethnic classification can wreak marks a shift from earlier categorization in taxonomically organized books like *Cimarron*. And like Fanny in *Fanny Herself*, Selina in *So Big*, Magnolia in *Show Boat*, and, of course, Ferber herself, Pansy internalizes her understanding of stagecraft from exposure to so many theatrical productions.

In her case, performance becomes a vehicle for racial depiction and performance. She and her mother see "Katie Putnam and Fanny Janauschek; they laughed at Callender's Colored Minstrels; they heard the Kentucky Jubilee Singers; they even ventured into the Chinese theater" (104). These were real people: Katie Putnam and Fannue Janauschek were famous actresses who toured the western states; Janauschek was Czech-born. Callender's Colored Minstrels were the actually African American minstrel arm of Callender's blackface performing empire, and the Kentucky Jubilee Singers were also a minstrel group. As in *Show Boat*, theater becomes a vehicle for various cultures as well as a place for Ferber to situate the empathetic Pansy at the junction of representation of actual history. Presentation becomes a pathway to actualization.

The prescient image of the stage also enters the novel through Lina Port, the pampered and citified New York actress who marries Vaughan and Pansy's son Dike. In contrast to Lina's powder-puff staginess, her African American employee projects authenticity: "Nothing of the comedy-stage maid about Hagar. A stately, imposing Negress, middle-aged, low-voiced; she looked and moved like an Egyptian queen in eyeglasses" (180). Hagar is presented as akin to the African American maid in *Come and Get It* who disabuses Dina Glasgow of her addled idea of Harlem as "orgiastic." Hagar, although a servant, evokes the centuries-old culture (in this case, Egyptian) that for Ferber is a shortcut to dignity and even, in Hagar's case, royalty. (Her Old Testament handmaid's name, however, underscores her status as a servant.) Contrasted with the "comedy-stage" portrayal of African Americans, and despite her employer's line of work, Hagar is no performer, no empty shell. She stands instead as a reproof to Lina's frivolous, shallow ways, and as a "real person."

Readers depended upon Ferber for such reality, finding in her characters portrayals that, despite their occasional literary heavy-handedness, nevertheless rang true. In 1939, a fan wrote to Ferber, pleading, "There is a story of America that you could write as no one else could. Write the story of the refugee Jews. But don't make them rich Jews, and don't preach" (Gilman 1939, 1). Heeding such calls, Ferber did her own part for real refugees as well as for fictional ones when she adopted a distantly related German Jewish family during World War II. They came to the United States, and Ferber supported them financially (Gilbert 1978, 249). And

Exact's servant, Reggie Dresden, functions as an almost exact response to the reader's request, neither rich nor preachy. Another of Ferber's overlooked Jewish characters, Reggie, a war refugee, has "[g]olden hair, neat and shining, unexpected warm brown eyes, clear blonde skin; slim, sturdy body" (1945, 75). Vaughan approves: "'Kind of a pretty name; got strength in it too, like her. Jewish, her folks are—or anyway were, back there in Germany, before Hitler killed them'" (75). With her fair appearance, Reggie provides a sharp contrast to other Jewish Ferber characters such as Ford in *The Girls* or Sol Levy in *Cimarron*, both of whom have dark skin and hair. With her it-could-happen-here blonde coloring and her American mother, Reggie demonstrates that refugees are not all the hollow-eyed starvelings America gaped at in war photos. "'We were nice, middle-class people who lived in a big pleasant flat full of beautiful things,'" she tells Mike (225). If a blonde half-American finds herself orphaned and persecuted by the war, the image of a "war refugee" alters significantly. Reggie defines herself against those who have "the walk of a concentration-camp prisoner. You walk like that when your spirit is broken. But there are many others of us who are still alive and eager" (229).

Mike's connection to Reggie irks Lina, who asks her son if he must "take out the hired help" (200). He retorts: "I'll try to get you her family tree, Maw, though I understand it's slightly bloodstained because her father and mother were murdered by the Nazis" (200). With impudent and righteous piety—"bloodstained" and "murdered" making a vehement point—Mike invokes Reggie's troubled past in order to vindicate her in defiance of his mother's insult. Although the Melendys use the pathos of Reggie's past as a constant point of reference, Reggie herself prefers to look only forward, saying, "When they let me have my papers and I am really an American citizen I never shall apologize and I never shall boast" (205). Unlike some of its senior citizens, such as Exact, who reaches back toward European-style feudalism, this refugee properly appreciates America, underlining why the country should welcome its newest citizens.

Mike, with the luxury of the American-born, alludes to a critical version of his own "bloodstained" local history, when white people "took the land and shoved [Indians] off it and herded them on a reservation— you know—kind of like a concentration camp.'" "'No! It isn't possible!'"

Reggie responds (211). Fresh from a world in which the concentration-camp analogy is not merely a rhetorical move, Reggie disbelieves such an impression would happen in America. The anti-Osage sentiments of a Sabra Cravat in *Cimarron* have evaporated in favor of stories about the Siwash Indians like Chief Seattle, representing a wronged people who remained strong even when horribly victimized. Mike's tone is occasionally patronizing—he tells Reggie that Chief Seattle "must have been quite a guy—not only for an Indian" (211)—but does not compare to the racist sentiments Sabra voices. Instead, the story of the Siwash nation becomes a vector for understanding and denouncing German anti-Semitism. It *can* happen here, Ferber tells her readers, and it did.

Mike and Reggie impose their new partnership on their now-shared city. They tour Seattle's market, noticing "Japanese girls, Japanese women, Japanese men . . . Scandinavians. Slavs. Irish. Italians. Fish, flesh, fowl, cheeses" (206). The "kaleidoscopic" mixture of various ethnic foods and vendors, harking back to the market where Selina sells her wares in *So Big*, accentuates Seattle as a site of vibrancy and diversity, emblematized by a profusion of intersecting identities that, like the foods they sell, are publicly available. At home, in contrast to Mike and Reggie's discovery, the Melendys' Japanese servants provide ethnic texture and a sense of foreboding: "Both Taka and his wife Masako . . . spoke English like Japanese stage servants, but their son William and their pretty daughter Grace, both American born, spoke without a trace of Japanese accent" (31). Ferber's recognition of the renamed May and Taka's performance-ready accents—which prove to read exactly like Dirk's Japanese butler's in *So Big*—gives an impression of ethnicity for an American audience. With their children's assimilative ability set against the theatrical nature of the parents, May and Taka become a symbol of the old America, an image being ushered out by cataclysmic world events.

The presence of these unaccented Tanakas demonstrates Ferber's evolution from depicting Asian Americans as caricatures (like Dirk's butler). William and Grace bear notably Anglo names and American speech. They not only seem assimilated because of these features, but because they cross both class and ethnicity lines to socialize with Mike, their peer. Even the generationally removed Vaughan internalizes this lesson when Emmy says,

"Those Japs are all alike."
"Nobody's all alike."
"What?"
"Nothing." (248)

With his "Nothing," Vaughan is unwilling to push his epiphany, but his retort signifies that he understands the dangers of casting individuals as representative of their ethnicity. Even he stretches tentatively toward understanding of a multiethnic America, pointing toward its inevitability.

Reggie's depiction of Jewish Europeans' shock at finding themselves Nazi targets sees a deliberate parallel in the Tanaka family's fate. As Reggie's family presumed in Germany—fair, half-American—the Tanakas feel safe, which accounts for their reactions when they understand the truth. (Ferber's insertion reflects upon her attempt to communicate her fears to Sulzberger.) As the report of the Japanese bombing of Pearl Harbor airs on the radio, Will attempts to seize Mike's airplane, and a birthday cake falls from Taka's hands in the dining room (271). The novel's narrative voice intones, "Taka and Masako and young Will and Grace were gone; they had been whisked away to a secret place, and Emmy said '. . . I always felt there was something I never did trust'" (273). With various retellings and reiterations of state-internalized persecution, *Great Son* traces a line from Indian reservations to concentration camps to internment camps. Emmy's proclamation of her long-time distrust, however dubious, furthers her xenophobia. She stands as a straw man, refusing to see the wrong in the internment of Japanese Seattle residents even when the horror-filled parallels are nakedly available.

Acting on his beliefs, Mike enlists, leaving a pregnant Reggie to work alongside Pansy in the factories. They marry over Emmy protesting that Mike is

"a Melendy and she's nobody and Jewish besides."
"Oh, she won't mind, Reggie won't. She's real democratic in her views. More than a good many American born. Besides, the Melendys need some new pioneer blood in the family. We're getting stale."
"Pioneer!"

"Well, sure. What she's gone through is worse than the Pilgrims,
and if she didn't come here to escape religious persecution I'd like to
know." (275–76)

Vaughan supports the wedding, which offers an opportunity to undo his
own doomed marriage as well as remedy the Melendy flaws in future generations. He himself grows from someone unwilling to push his mother
in her closed-mindedness to a champion of Mike's youthful idealism. His
joke about Reggie being "real democratic" in her views even as his wife
demonstrates her continued bigotry demonstrates that, rather than envi-
sioning her ethnicity and religion as a drawback, Vaughan situates Reggie's being "Jewish besides" as a particularly American feature, aligning
her with the pilgrims who fled religious persecution to come to America,
people in whose image Exact considers herself. Furthering the family
split, Exact gives Reggie some valuable jewelry, cementing the idea that
Reggie is an appropriate choice to carry on the family name, as well as
returning heirlooms to someone whose were stolen.

With its chaotic finale—war, babies, elders defied and new blood on
the way—*Great Son* concludes open-endedly, leaving the reader to wonder if Mike survives the war. Yet the image of the baby who will carry on
his and Reggie's heritage bolsters the idea of "new pioneer blood" keeping
the old Melendy strain from "staleness." The future is a mixed blessing, a
child who bears the legacies both of the Melendys and the Dresdens, rob-
bers and refugees, and will add yet another shard of color to the quickly
moving kaleidoscope of Seattle.

After the hectic conclusion of *Great Son*, Ferber turned to *Giant*,
which the last chapter situated as putting forth another vision of a mixed
America residing in its youngest inhabitants and inheritors of a formi-
dable dynasty. Like *Giant*, her final novel, *Ice Palace*, also deals with a vast
land: Alaska. Ferber recognized the parallels between Alaska and Texas;
as one Alaskan character says, "'We're worse than the Texans'" (1958,
230). *Ice Palace* had a more than metaphoric role in turning Alaska into
a state. The novel was published in 1958, and Alaska became a state in
1959, which many involved agreed was no coincidence. As Ernest Gruening, Alaska's first governor, writes in his book *The Battle for Alaska
Statehood*:

I had gotten Edna to write this book which followed an acquaintance we had struck up some years before. . . . Having been an admirer of her fiction for some years, I suggested to her that she ought to write a novel about Alaska. . . . *Ice Palace* made a strong case, in fiction form, for statehood. Some of the literary critics felt it was not up to her best work but one of them referred to it quite correctly as "the *Uncle Tom's Cabin* for Alaska statehood." (1967, 102)

In other words, Ferber's work assisted in the creation of a state. Gruening's point about literary critics speaks to the idea that Ferber's novels work on different levels, that a middlebrow book with over-the-top coincidences, descriptions, and plots can function also as an argument for something as crucial and basic to America as statehood. As a final work and salvo, the novel-into-state transition suited Ferber perfectly. She literally helped to fashion a piece of America.

With *Ice Palace* Ferber takes a step beyond the theme of racial mixture as primarily a harbinger of the future—as in *Great Son* and *Giant*—to depict a society already vibrant with ethnically blended characters. This hybridity is primarily represented by the elementally named Christine Storm, *Ice Palace*'s protagonist, who recalls *Saratoga Trunk*'s Clio Dulaine with her ineffably intermingled—and extraordinarily attractive—appearance. In a parody of the old "but you don't look Jewish" expression, Christine hears "'You certainly don't look like an Alaskan'" (1958, 6). At first, it appears that Ferber employs this parallel to highlight the inanity and ludicrousness of such comments, but she undermines any such pointedness when she writes: "But then, even the girl's appearance had a touch of incredibility. Her eyes were black, her hair golden. Baffled by the unusual combination, strangers assumed that the yellow hair was tinted. . . . The skin warmly golden" (7). With passages like this, Ferber maintains the inability to categorize Christine's beauty—much like that of the also dark-eyed and light-haired Reggie Dresden—with her diction of incredibility and bafflement. Christine's beauty is almost super-human, made up of only the loveliest, most unearthly parts of her Caucasian and Eskimo forbears.

In this final frontier of America, the last remnant of its relentless westward push, Christine's grandfather Thor takes Christine on a trip around the territory at a pace that suggests to her that he is "running a race with something" and gives the novel its hectic progress (180). The loftily and authoritatively named Thor, who like his namesake acts as a heavy-handed god of his surroundings, wants Christine to see the most "primitive" villages, demonstrating his respect for the past and the purity of the way in which native peoples live as well as his dreams for the next generation:

> Soon, there won't be an actual Eskimo left—that is, an Eskimo with no Caucasian strain. Long ago the Russian and the Scandinavian and the English explorers and hunters and whalers took the Eskimo women. Then the American gold hunters. And now the new rush of construction workers, the technicians, the flyers, the lonely men in the army bases, isolated. The whole modern crew. It ought to make a pretty good specimen of America. It has, through the years. You know—the mixture as before. (173)

Thor's speech itself works as the "pretty good specimen": he mentions covering the myriad ways in which identities are shaped, from loneliness to modernity. But even Thor, a resolute newspaperman bent on Alaskan statehood, sees that the days of ethnic reductiveness—when an Eskimo and an American were two different categories—are over, and his "race" is run. Dewey's hyphens have arrived. He modifies his phrase "actual Eskimo" with the "that is" portion of the sentence. He knows that there will be no use for the phrase "actual Eskimo" in a future in which separate bloodlines are no longer curated.

Further ethnic interrogation adds Jewishness to the Alaskan landscape through a dinner-party anecdote, in which a man named Gilhooley is a missionary priest and new pilot who becomes distressed when forbidden to land:

> "God's sake what'll I do?"
> "Repeat after me: 'Yisgadal v'yishkaddash sh'meg rabbo, b'olmo d'vro kir'useh v'yamlich malchuseh, b'chaycecon uv'yomechon uv'chayeh d'chol bes yisroel—'"
> Mead Haskell broke off into helpless laughter in which Ross joined. The others wore the resentful expression of the uncomprehending.

> "Very funny and all, I don't doubt," Bridie said, crisply. "But maybe
> if we knew what it meant it would seem funnier" (143)

The joke is that the ground controller is giving the priest the Jewish Kaddish, or prayer for the dead, as if he is bound to crash. (Gilhooley lives.) But Ferber's larger joke is that the controller would be Jewish in the first place, that someone managing the airplanes at Oogruk, Alaska, gives a prayer so outlandish that both the principals in the story and the dinner guests years later believe that it is nothing more than a stream of gibberish. "If we knew what it meant," Chris's maternal friend Bridie says, and she could be speaking for both Father Gilhooley and everyone who does not know the old story. Ross's laughter places him with the Jewish ground controller and the old Alaskans who "get it." To him, a joke based on lack of understanding across a cultural divide includes the key ingredients for humor. A missionary named Gilhooley is clearly not schooled in Hebrew prayer, and would miss the mordant humor of the anecdote, just as Bridie's "resentful expression" demonstrates the quick acrimony that humor can engender if it is targeted only at one specific group; in this case, the people who knew and liked the story versus those who could not understand the punch line. More pointedly, the joke demonstrates the layered slippage between outsider and insider in Alaska, where a Jewish ground controller can jibe a missionary in a way only he (the controller), presumably, could understand, and then have the account be retold as a multilayered joke at a gathering years later. That Father Gilhooley survives both the airplane landing and the ribbing from ground control testifies to the pluck of the Alaskan, no matter his origin.

Actual Jewishness means more to Alaska than dinner conversation, however. The Raffsky family of Oogruk live in the depths of Alaska, but maintain a stereotypically New York type of Jewish urbanity. The son, Norman, "looked vaguely Columbia University sophomore whose highly solvent father (in the wholesale dress manufacturing business) pampers him" (219). The most locally specific and urban terms—situated in New York City's Columbia University—apply to these far-flung people. Norman's father, Isador Raffsky, experiences a fairly typical Jewish-peddler trajectory, similar to that of Sol Levy in *Cimarron*: "He looked like a thousand other compact shrewd and friendly men standing at the doors of their shops in Fargo, North Dakota, and Houston, Texas, and Cleveland, Ohio, and Appleton, Wisconsin" (221). (Appleton, of course, was one of the towns in which Ferber's father would have stood in the doorway of his own store.) Turning Isador into an everyman Jewish merchant—"compact shrewd and friendly"—accentuates the way in which Alaska can be read as an American microcosm, complete with Jewish storekeeper.

Like their brother and with similarly local—New York—imagery, Isador's daughters highlight the contrast in the novel between more typical representations of Jewish culture and commonly held ideas about Alaska. They "were like two nice plump upper Bronx girls you might see having a ice-cream soda at Schrafft's at five, now transported, incongruously, to the frigid wilderness of the Bering Sea" (225). The tension inherent in ethnic classification lurks within in the Raffsky girls' "incongruous" appearance, because Ferber's other descriptions of Alaska lead readers to expect air-traffic controllers who recite the Hebrew Kaddish and a storekeeper named Raffsky. In the diverse world she depicts, two Schrafft's-bound teenagers seem as predictable as anyone else, except that they are termed "incongruous." With this disconnect, Ferber continues the slippage with which she grapples throughout *Ice Palace*. If Alaska—or America—is a model of ethnic mixture, is it truly surprising for the Raffsky girls to be Alaskan?

If Chris's reaction to the Raffskys is indicative, the answer is yes. Meeting them, "Chris now said hi in turn and was conscious of a slightly dazed feeling, inured though she had been since birth to the incongruities of Alaska" (224). The return of the word "incongruous" signals that Jewishness can render the typically dauntless Chris "slightly dazed." Even though Chris herself is put forth as an organically successful mixture of Eskimo and white progenitors, the Raffskys still represent difference. Chris investigates the family further, seeing Mrs. Leah Raffsky's "mysterious" appearance, inherent in her facial features: "By some inexplicable alchemy of the centuries Leah Raffsky's darkly luminous slanting eyes, her high cheekbones curving down to the delicately sensuous mouth . . . all might have been copied complete from ancient Egyptian royalty" (223). Chris's mystification is answered by the cultural venerability that Leah embodies, since she is a true "Oriental" by the standards of Ferber's earlier writing. Isador explains further: "'Leah's mother was half Eskimo.

. . . And what do you think [her father] was? A rabbi! Did you ever hear before of such a thing!'" (229). Even Isador internalizes the incredibility of his family's existence. Given her background, Leah's marrying a Jewish man privileges the Jewish half of her heritage, so that she produces a Columbia sophomore and two Schrafft's customers instead of a Chris Storm or a Ross Guildenstern. With Ferber's repeated "incongruity," *Ice Palace* seems to indicate that Jewishness, not Alaska, is the final frontier that cannot be entirely assimilated. Interestingly, Leah Raffsky was apparently based upon a real woman, Clara Rotman Salinas, born Clara Levy in 1914 in the nearby village of Kiana. Her father, an accountant named William Shakespeare Levy, came to Alaska during the Klondike Gold Rush, shortly after 1900. Levy's wife had died, and he raised four Alaskan daughters as Jews. Like Leah Raffsky, Clara operated general stores, both still extant.[1]

Like Clara Levy's, Leah Raffsky's Jewishness pushes to the forefront. Ferber draws a sharp parallel between the Jews and the Eskimos. Ross takes some tourists to an Eskimo dance, and explains that "'[t]ribal stories never are very interesting.'" (228). Thor remonstrates, "'The Bible is largely made up of tribal tales told first by word of mouth through hundreds of years'" (237). History creates authority. Eskimo tribal dances, complicated by their being performed for tourists instead of maintained as a cultural insider's ritual, gain as much relevance as Bible stories in Thor's replacement formulation. Ferber never terms the Eskimos "Oriental," but the benison of history nevertheless shades them as important. Chris joins the dancers, and becomes indistinguishable "except, perhaps, for the shining gold mass of her hair" (238). This one detail remains inassimilable, her fair hair marking her difference from the other dancers, even though her blood ties her to them and to a noble—near-Biblical and oriental—history.

The dual pull on Chris from the picturesque culture and its dashing representative, Ross, provokes Bridie: "'Do you think that Eskimo boy is good enough for our Chris! Do you?'" (255). Bridie is "horrified" once she remembers Thor's Eskimo and Chris's resultant Eskimo heritage. The episode serves to emphasize Chris's perfection as a symbol of Alaska, since she possesses the rare ability to (almost) blend in with the dancers,

1. So reports Mark S. Glickman in a 2002 article in *Reform Judaism Magazine* (2002, 71).

while remaining palatable to white Alaskans like Bridie, who can continue to harbor ethnocentric assumptions, and even to forget that Chris is an Eskimo. Contradictions persist, despite and because of Ferber's rhetoric. Ferber's willingness to leave some "incongruities" remarkable lends support to the idea of a country still in possession of a frontier, a place continuously in motion.

In fact, as Bridie's (sometimes) repressed bigotry suggests, Thor's Alaska, however, is no utopia, but contains within its vibrantly melded culture racial anxiety and a characteristically colonial hierarchy. Asked why he doesn't fly a passenger plane instead of a freighter, Ross responds, "'Eskimo, I guess'" (171), implying that his race provokes hirers to pass him over for more prestigious assignments. Too, the difference and ethnic blending that Alaska brings strains families as well as individuals. Ferber describes a typical family reunion: "Dark slanting eyes in a startlingly pink-and-white face might regard gravely a gray-haired grandmother whose spare New England figure sat so erect beside the daughter-in-law and the grandchild that she now was seeing and visiting in a daze of unbelief," an apprehension that works both ways as the daughter-in-law "thought this old lady, her husband's mother, must be a strange one!" (176). The image of the "spare" New Englander—the bitter great-aunts of *So Big*, the problematic forbears of *American Beauty*—collides with the mixed or Native wife to produce a mutual "daze of unbelief" that both recalls Chris's impression of the Raffskys and accompanies Thor's vision of the future: the mixed-race baby, whose coloring evokes Chris's, the face of what is yet to come in Ferber's march of mixed identities.

Thor seeks ethnonyms for the superior hybrids—the baby, Chris, Ross—he counts on Alaska to produce. "First thing you know, we'll have an Eskimo strain president of the United States. . . . Tough stuff, mongrels. Usually nimble in the mind and on the feet. Look at all those dark-skinned black-haired brown-eyed Englishmen of Cornwall. Even after five years, when the Spanish Armada was wrecked off the English coast" (174). Reaching back into European history to find examples of the vigor of mixed-blood people invokes Ferber's time-honored and Jewishly informed method of legitimizing a culture through its history while allowing Thor to predict success for his beloved territory. Instead of Orientals, Thor employs the figure of the sailors of the Spanish Armada. Despite the slippage that the Raffskys' existence presents, Ferber's formulation seems to point toward an eventual theoretical alignment of Alaskans with Jews, in the sense that an august past—preferably one including some genetic "tough stuff"—portends an honorable future, full of accomplishment and fertile continuation of the new "strain."

Ross—significantly an insider in the Father Gilhooley/Jewish prayer joke's audience—represents the example of healthy and seemly mixture, the hale Alaskan fit to take control, yet still fighting for work as whiter men are hired. Thor says that Eskimos are dying off because they have been "killed by civilization" (173). Thor concedes to Chris:

> "Yes, the breeds survive pretty well. That mixture of Eskimo and Scandinavian stock, or German or English or American. That is pretty sturdy stuff."
>
> "Like me." (173)

Once all of Alaska is "like me," or like Chris, its future will be secure. Dewey's hyphens not only will connect, but form the only descriptions of Alaskans available. The Alaska of *Ice Palace* represents a place of change and dynamism, but in Thor's formulation, the energy must move toward ethnically hybrid Alaskans like Ross and Chris. The "actual Eskimo," according to Thor, is an anachronism, left behind as the "breeds" survive and forge ahead.

As her grandfather does, Chris consistently looks to the future on her tour of Alaska, admiring the women representatives of the Alaska legislature and listening as Thor lists the ethnically variegated names on the rosters, including Gunderson, O'Shaughnessy, and Utokok: "'That's not so different, is it? That's like every other place in the United States, isn't it?' 'My darling girl!'" (175). Without guile, Christine manages to make Alaska part of the country and accept with Thor-gratifying nonchalance the heterogeneity he strives to foster for her. Her understated, almost childlike, belief that all of America is as vigorously mixed as her own territory enshrines her as the arrival of the future, an unjaded representative with the same pink cheeks and brown eyes of the baby on the plane.

The vivifying effect of such characters leads to the impassioned pleas for statehood that the novel delivers, panegyrics that derail the narrative but seem to have achieved their author's purpose in an incredibly real way when Alaska did indeed become one of the United States. Thor could be delivering a speech to American citizens—and is notably in Isador Raffksy's company, allying the Jewish character with his own fervor—when he proclaims: "'This is the new Alaska,' Thor said. . . . 'We knew the old one, didn't we, Isador? It's gone. This is your Alaska, Christine. Take over'" (223). Thor pushes the territory toward the next generation, making statehood the responsibility of strong mixed Alaskans like Chris and Ross. With "his" Alaska "gone," the future, as it is in *Giant*, is present.

When the nonfictional Alaska actually became a state, many agreed at least partially due to the arguments inherent within *Ice Palace*, Ferber had literally created a piece of America. The book had contributed to something far larger than itself, or even Ferber's library of work. Her many years of researching, imagining, and portraying America had taken her to the frontier, where new formulations awaited her. Her concentration, toward the end of her life, on spaces containing such a wide proliferation of ethnicities proved a natural culmination for a career dedicated to an understanding of the complex space of America through its ethnic identities and the intersections at which they met, overlapped, and moved on, irrevocably altered.

Ferber's involvement in Alaskan statehood in all its near-unbelievable grandiosity provides an appropriate finale for her work, which so relentlessly sought to survey and define American places. Ferber's regional novels naturally represent her authorial development and her inward- and outward-looking understanding of the country she depicted. These works demonstrate a unique understanding of the American cultural landscape. Her novels, still difficult to categorize, grapple with identity issues that have long engrossed any chronicler of this uniquely configured and constantly shifting country.

Ferber's books took on an increasingly complex matrix of racial, ethnic, and international identities to form a continuum of American portrayals. In *Dawn O'Hara*, Ferber experimented with ethnicity while staying safely within gradations of whiteness—Irish, Welsh, German. The plot was dramatic, but the racial navigations remained minor, ranging closely within a confined category of ethnicity. *Dawn O'Hara* demonstrated nevertheless the ethnically bounded way in which Ferber envisioned America, and that she maintained an interest in pushing not just gender boundaries, but ethnic taxonomies as well.

Her concern with ethnicities gave rise to the frankly autobiographical novel *Fanny Herself*, in which Ferber built upon what she had begun with *Dawn O'Hara* to produce a novel that gave her room to consider the Jewish identity that had most affected her own life. Within its economy, Ferber probed questions of belonging, bigotry, passing, and whiteness, all integral to her own understanding and experience of life as a Jewish girl and young woman in turn-of-the-century Wisconsin. Ferber's stand-in, Fanny, ultimately finds her own way of being Jewish, moving through a period of unease with Jewishness, and finally learning to balance authenticity with the special "Oriental" brand of special and elevated Jewishness that she fulfills through art.

Ferber's next book, the Chicago-based *The Girls*, is not so focused upon Jewish issues, but builds upon the idea of the urban experience and the attendant heterogeneity she had framed with *Dawn O'Hara's* Milwaukee. Although shallowly plotted, *The Girls*, like *Dawn O'Hara*, delves into the life of one city to expose its ethnic and societal disquiet. Here as well, Ferber uses the Jewish character Ford to bring into focus the importance of classification to the societal organization of a city, even as she indicts bigotry through an exposition of its absurdity when viewed through the lens of the rapidity of the American rags-to-riches myth. Her *Girls* learn that America demands resilience, and that class assignment matters because the very challenging of it forges ingenuity within a social as well as historical frame. As variously ethnic characters—Jewish and Slavic among them—struggle to reinvent themselves, Chicago expands and unfolds. In fact, that city preoccupied Ferber so much that her 1924 novel, *So Big*, remains there, enlarging upon themes of *The Girls*. Within its own rags-to-riches story, *So Big* evinces a more expansive and sophisticated view of the city as well as the additional layering of class and urban/rural tensions, sharpened by questions of the importance of artistic achievement. *So Big* confronts the question of balance, both in individual lives and in the larger community, by confronting topics from blackface minstrelsy to visual artistry. With this articulate novel, Ferber puts forth a more mature—and vexed—vision of what ethnic and visionary mixture can mean.

In the 1926 *Show Boat,* Ferber pressed further upon questions of African American identity that recall the performance-saturated imagery circulating around African American identity in *So Big. Show Boat* remains Ferber's most famous, parsed, and considered text because of the multiple ways it has been produced on stage and screen, and Ferber's scrutiny of the contemporary American scheme of overlapping races and regions explodes preexisting binaries to expose the problematical striation of racial division and categorization. The novel accomplishes all this through a lens of carnivalesque stagings and performances, which throw into relief the increasingly complex, weighted way in which Ferber was considering the manufacture of American ethnicity.

By the time *Cimarron* was published in 1929, Ferber had sharpened her focus on the heart of the American story: the westering pioneer. Like the plains she considered, her work became larger, and more expansive. An in-depth study of how a piece of the West was founded, Ferber's dizzying story of an Oklahoma family plunged into a new life forces questions of what constitutes resistance and collusion as alliances shift, forged into difference by ethnicities familiar to Ferber's earlier works—Jewishness and African Americanness—and realigned and reimagined through the presence of the Osage people who live in Oklahoma and create another template for reevaluating American authenticity and entitlement. It also created a preoccupation with the creation of America that worked on a literal level as Oklahoma went from territory to state, but also on a level of imagery and nationhood. Ferber's work raised the question of who desires the title of American and began to arrive at multivalent conclusions, all pointing toward the concept of mixed ethnicities as crucial components to viable nationhood.

With the 1932 *American Beauty,* Ferber confronted and upended another American myth, that of New England as the hallowed American birthplace. Returning to some of the performance-delineated intersections used in *Showboat* and to a lesser extent in *So Big* and *Cimarron,* Ferber reframes some cherished figures and imagery. Exposing the turbulence endemic to a new immigrant population—Polish people in this case—*American Beauty* may be Ferber's most self-consciously literary work. Within the novel, Ferber turns the notion of the industrious white Puritans inside out. *American Beauty* uses an undercurrent of gothic deformity, embodied both in individuals and the landscape, and less than human characters constructing their identities within and without competing discourses of Americanness. Ferber's deliberate rendering of the clean white landscape of Puritan America into a decaying society in need of renovation and new immigrant blood points toward a newly multifaceted portrait of the nation. *American Beauty* reveals further entrenched engagement with the American past as Ferber synthesized history with the future and former terms of ethnicity with their potential outcomes and definitions.

Come and Get It, published in 1934, mirrors *American Beauty* in some aspects. It contains a similar trajectory to that of the land-proud Orrange family, and it includes the specter of downward mobility and dissolution. *Come and Get It,* however, more fully navigates class and its relationship to industrialism and land ownership. With more polemical characters and a sidebar of European life contrasting with American, Ferber continued to tease out issues of whiteness in a discourse suggesting that within such minute classifications as Scotch-Irish and Polish lay the underpinnings of a plural America. Without the blood of a text like *Cimarron,* but its own brand of pathos, *Come and Get It* nevertheless demonstrated the subterranean forces that could shape or hinder America, including environmentalism and a Whitmanesque celebration of the individual. Fewer ethnicities are at play, but the increased pressure upon construction of "the American" suggests further scrutiny and rumination on American ethnicity.

In some ways, *Saratoga Trunk* seemed a regression. The 1941 novel retreats from the ever-burgeoning West back to the East Coast. A sort of revision of *Show Boat,* preoccupied with matters of race and the South, *Saratoga Trunk* also addresses the conflation of staginess, stagecraft, and African Americanness. It differs significantly from the earlier novel in that Ferber imagines a world where the forces are no less dire, but within which the various cogencies could be marshaled for success rather than simply resigned to predestined tragedy. With a more complex cast of characters, and set against the background of an over-wealthy class of American, Ferber's Saratoga enmeshes many earlier themes from passing to the carnivalesque moments of *American Beauty* to put forth a romantic and multilayered story of performance validity that underlines, once again, the importance of plural identities for a vibrant, productive society.

With the 1952 *Giant,* Ferber finally left the image of the stage behind. Instead, she set her novel on the bare earth of Texas and imagined a world focused by family and framed by race. *Giant,* with echoes of *Cimarron,* understands the cowboy myth and its impact on real America; here, especially upon Mexican Americans. Ferber had come to a point of re-envisioning her own work. With this writerly consciousness, she renovated and pushed some of her most crucial themes into further productivity and fullness, until one family, synthesized by history and time, unites for an intricate but somehow less despondent view of America than that which underlies some of her earlier work. With *Great Son* and *Ice Palace,* Ferber examined and exposed the ways in which definitions of ethnicity form cultures and affect individuals, understanding all the while that these designations mutate and shift depending upon vantage point, understanding, and time.

In the introduction to their *Insider/Outsider: American Jews and Multiculturalism,* Biale, Galchinsky, and Hesche write that Jews "represent that boundary case whose very lack of belonging to a recognizable category creates a sense of unease" (1998, 5). As a Jew, grounded in her own background and experiences navigating America, Ferber forced that unease to its limits, using her own lack of belonging to sharpen and add texture to the often-vexed gaze that shapes her fiction. The result was a body of novels in which Ferber offers no one view of her intricate world, but puts forth a vision of a place in which relentless ethnic negotiation forms a foundational part of culture. The novels present narratives saturated with ethnicity and identity politics, economies within which individual characters embody stereotypes even as they evade and explode them. Ferber's articulation of an ethnically manifold America adds another—crucial—dimension to her already sweeping written portraits. Ferber not only spent a literary lifetime writing about her country, but through her novels, she combined her original outsider status with a more interior, personal view. Within the economies of her regional novels, she considered and internalized the various ethnicities about which she wrote, and envisioned a time when their blending would necessarily mean the end of some of the stratified categorization that plagued the world as she saw it. As she wrote, simply, of her America: "It is the one country I really understand" (1939, 9).

Works Cited

Adams, Franklin P. "Faulkner and Ferber." N.d., n.p. Edna Ferber Papers, Wisconsin Historical Society, Box 8.

Antler, Joyce. *The Journey Home: Jewish Women and the American Century.* New York: Free P, 1997.

Avery, Eileen, ed. *Modern Jewish Writers in America.* New York: Macmillan, 2007.

Balz, Dan, and Haynes Johnson. "A Political Odyssey." *Washington Post.* Aug. 2, 2009, A1.

Bartlett, John. *Bartlett's Familiar Quotations.* Boston: Little, Brown, 1992.

Batker, Carol. "Literary Reformers: Crossing Class and Ethnic Boundaries in Jewish Women's Fiction of the 1920s." *MELUS* 25. 1 (Spring 2000): 81–104.

———. *Reforming Fictions: Native, African, and Jewish American Women's Literature and Journalism in the Progressive Era.* New York: Columbia UP, 2000.

Bennett, Juda P. *The Passing Figure.* New York: Peter Lang, 1996.

Berlant, Lauren. *The Female Complaint: The Unfinished Business of Sentimentality in American Culture.* Durham: Duke UP, 2008.

Biale, David, Michael Galchinsky, and Susannah Heschel, eds. *Insider/Outsider: American Jews and Multiculturalism.* Berkeley: California UP, 1998.

Boelhower, William Q. *The Future of American Modernism: Ethnic Writing Between the Wars.* Amsterdam, Netherlands: VU UP, 1990.

Botshon, Lisa, and Meredith Goldsmith, eds. *Middlebrow Moderns: Popular Women Writers of the 1920s.* Boston: Northeastern UP, 2003.

Boydston, Jo Ann., ed. *The Middle Works of John Dewey 1899–1924.* Carbondale: Southern Illinois UP, 2008.

Brainerd, Betty. "Among The Lumberjacks." *Brooklyn Daily Eagle.* Feb. 24, 1935. www.fultonhistory.com. Accessed Feb. 23, 2012.

Brandeis, Louis D. *A Call To The Educated Jew. Menorah Journal* 1.1: 13–19.

Breon, Robin. "Show Boat: The Revival, The Racism." *Drama Review* 39.2 (Summer 1995): 86–105.

Brindze, Ruth. "Edna Ferber Writes Fiction Because She Can't Help Herself." *Brooklyn Daily Eagle*. 1924. www.fultonhistory.com. Accessed Feb. 23, 2012.

Brown, William Wells. *Clotel*. 1853. New York: Penguin, 2003.

Bruccoli, Matthew. *F. Scott Fitzgerald in the Marketplace*. Columbia: South Carolina UP, 2009.

Burrough, Bryan. *The Big Rich: The Rise and Fall of the Greatest Texas Oil Fortunes*. New York: Penguin, 2009.

Campbell, Donna. "'Written with a Hard and Ruthless Purpose': Rose Wilder Lane, Edna Ferber, and Middlebrow Regional Fiction." In Botshon and Goldsmith 2003, 25–44.

Chamberlain, John. "Books of the Times." *New York Times*. Feb. 20, 1935, 17.

Cheyette, Bryan. *Between "Race" and Culture*. Palo Alto: Stanford UP, 1996.

Clark, Suzanne. *Sentimental Modernism: Women Writers and the Revolution of the Word*. Bloomington: Indiana UP, 1991.

"Critical Reviews of the Season's Latest Fiction." *New York Sun*. Oct. 6, 1917. 6.

Currie, George. "Passed in Review." *Brooklyn Daily Eagle*. Aug. 25, 1926. www.fultonhistory.com. Accessed Feb. 23, 2012.

Dewey, John. "Nationalizing Education." 1916. In Boydston 2008, 205.

Dickens, Charles. *The Old Curiosity Shop*. [1841]. New York: Penguin, 1984.

Dickinson, Rogers. *Edna Ferber: A Sketch*. New York: Doubleday, Doran, and Co., 1925.

Downing, Hilda. "Ferber Writes of Oklahoma." *Tulsa Tribune*. N.d. Edna Ferber Papers, Appleton Library.

"Edna Ferber Sails For Europe Tonight." *New York Times*. Aug. 12, 1932. 12.

Felski, Rita. *The Gender of Modernity*. Cambridge, MA: Harvard UP, 1995.

Ferber, Edna. *American Beauty*. New York: Doubleday, 1931.

———. *Cimarron*. New York: Doubleday, 1929.

———. *Come and Get It*. New York: Doubleday, 1934.

———. *Dawn O'Hara*. [1911]. New York: Stokes, 1938.

———. "The Fenced-In Reservoir." *New York Times*. Mar. 16, 1926. 24.

———. *Emma McChesney and Co.* [1915]. Chicago: U of Chicago P, 2001.

———. *Fanny Herself.* [1917]. Chicago: U of Chicago P, 2001.

———. *Giant*. New York: Doubleday, 1952.

———. *Gigolo*. New York: Doubleday, 1922.

———. *The Girls*. New York: Doubleday, 1921.

———. *Great Son*. New York: Doubleday, 1945.

———. *Ice Palace*. [1958]. New York: Fawcett, 1971.

———. *A Kind of Magic*. New York: Lancer, 1963.

———. "My Son, The Show Boat." *New York Times*. July 17, 1966. 73.

———. *No Room at the Inn.* New York: Doubleday, 1941.

———. "Nobody's in Town." New York: Avon, 1944.

———. *A Peculiar Treasure.* New York: Doubleday, 1939.

———. *Personality Plus.* [1914]. Chicago: U of Chicago P, 2001.

———. *Roast Beef, Medium.* [1913]. Chicago: U of Chicago P, 2001.

———. *Saratoga Trunk.* [1941]. New York: Harper Collins, 2000.

———. *Show Boat.* [1926]. New York: Signet, 1994.

———. *So Big.* New York: Doubleday, 1924.

"Ferber Fundamentals." *Time.* Feb. 5, 1945. www.time.com/time/magazine/article /0,9171,797104,00.html. Accessed Sept. 19, 2009.

Fitzgerald, F. Scott. *The Great Gatsby.* [1925]. New York: Scribner, 1980.

Frederick, John T. "Speaking of Books." *The Rotarian.* May 1945. 34–36.

Geraghty. Christine. *Now a Major Motion Picture: Film Adaptations of Literature and Drama.* New York: Rowman and Littlefield, 2008.

Gilbert, Julie. *Ferber: Edna Ferber and Her Circle.* New York: Applause, 1978.

Gilman, Barbara. Letter to Edna Ferber. May 7, 1939. Edna Ferber Papers, Wisconsin Historical Society, Box 6, Folder 9.

Gislason, Eric. "Edna Ferber's *Ice Palace*: The Uncle Tom's Cabin of Alaska Statehood." Available at the U of Virginia's American Studies site. xroads.virginia .edu/~cap/BARTLETT/palace.html. Accessed July 2, 2008.

Glickman, Mark. "The Ice Rebbe Cometh." *Reform Judaism* 31.1 (Fall 2002). www.reformjudaismmag.net/02fall/icerebbe.shtml. Accessed Nov. 27, 2009.

Goddu, Teresa. *Gothic America.* New York: Columbia UP, 1997.

Gruening, Ernest. *The Battle for Alaska Statehood.* Seattle: U of Washington P, 1967.

Hart, James D. *The Popular Book: A History of America's Literary Taste.* Berkeley: California UP, 1961.

Hughes, Langston. "Some Practical Observations: A Colloquy." *Phylon* 11.4 (1950): 307–11.

Ifkovic, Ed. *Lone Star: An Edna Ferber Mystery.* Scottsdale: Poisoned Pen P, 2009.

Junegst, William. "Today's Books." *Brooklyn Eagle.* Oct. 5, 1952. www.fultonhistory .com. Accessed Jan. 16, 2012.

Kalmar, Ivan Davidson, and Derek J. Penslar. "Orientalism and the Jews: An Introduction." In Kalmar and Penslar 2005, xiii–xl.

———, eds. *Orientalism and the Jews.* Waltham: Brandeis UP, 2005.

Kanaga, Heidi. "Edna Ferber's *Cimarron*, Cultural Authority, and 1920s Western Historical Narratives." In Botshon and Goldsmith 2003, 167–202.

Kilmer, Joyce. "Business Woman Most Domestic." *New York Times.* Apr. 4, 1915. SM4–5.

Kreuger, Miles. *Show Boat: The Story of a Classic American Musical.* New York: Da Capo, 1977.

Kubiak, H. J. Letter to Edna Ferber. Sept. 24, 1934. Edna Ferber Papers, Wisconsin Historical Society, Box 6, Folder 1.

Lichtenstein, Diane. *Writing Their Nations: The Tradition of Nineteenth-Century American Jewish Writers.* Bloomington: Indiana UP, 1992.

Lott, Eric. *Love and Theft: Blackface Minstrelsy and the American Working Class.* New York: Oxford UP, 1995.

Lutes, Jean Marie. *Front Page Girls: Women Journalists in American Culture and Fiction, 1880–1930.* New York: Cornell UP, 2006.

Marcus, Jacob Rader. *The American Jewish Woman: A Documentary History.* New York: Ktav, 1981.

Marks, Peter. "Daring to Do a Texas-Size Task: Create a 'Giant' of Note." *Washington Post.* May 10, 2009. www.washingtonpost.com/wp-dyn/content/article/2009/05/07/AR2009050704597_2.html. Accessed June 24, 2012.

Marsh, Fred T. "Edna Ferber's 'Come And Get It." *New York Times Book Review.* Feb. 24, 1935. 6.

Meade, Marion. *Bobbed Hair and Bathtub Gin: Writers Running Wild in the Twenties.* New York: Harcourt, 2004.

"Miss Ferber Answers New England Critics." *New York Times.* Jan. 12, 1932. 21.

"Miss Ferber's Vivid Tale of Oklahoma's Settling." *New York Times Book Review.* Mar. 23, 1930. 3.

Mitchell, Margaret. *Gone With the Wind.* [1936]. New York: Simon and Schuster, 2008.

Mullett, Mary B. "Who's Who Among Women of Big Achievement." *Washington Herald.* Mar. 13, 1914. 8.

Nichols, Lewis. "Talk With Edna Ferber." *New York Times Book Review.* Oct. 5, 1952. 30.

Offit, Sidney. *Friends, Writers, and Other Countrymen: A Memoir.* New York: St. Martin's P, 2008.

Peterson, Carla. *Doers of the Word.* 1995. New York: Oxford UP.

Raub, Patricia. *Yesterday's Stories: Popular Women's Novels of the Twenties and Thirties.* Westport, CT: Greenwood P, 1994.

Rubin, Joan Shelley. *The Making of Middlebrow Culture.* Chapel Hill: North Carolina UP, 1992.

Shapiro, Ann. "Edna Ferber: Jewish American Feminist." *Shofar: An Interdisciplinary Journal of Jewish Studies* 20.2 (2002): 52–60.

———. "When Edna Ferber Was Accused of Communist Propaganda." *Studies in American Jewish Literature* 27 (2008): 16–22.

Smyth, J. E. *Edna Ferber's Hollywood*. Texas UP, 2010.

Sutton, Fred E. Letter. Apr. 10, 1929. Edna Ferber Papers, Appleton Library, Box 5.

"3 Liners Dock." *New York Tribune*. Sept. 4, 1922. www.fultonhistory.com. Accessed Apr. 10, 2012.

Thompson, Ralph. "Books of the Times." *New York Times*. Nov. 6, 1941. 21.

Van de Water, Frederic. "Edna Ferber Deals Robustly With Truth." *New York Evening Post*. Oct. 31, 1931. 7.

Wallace, Margaret. "A Connecticut Pageant By Miss Ferber." *New York Times Book Review*. Oct. 18, 1931. 7.

Walzer, Michael. "Multiculturalism and the Politics of Interest." In Biale, Galchinsky, and Heschel, 88–98.

Watts, Eileen. "Edna Ferber, Jewish American Writer: Who Knew?" In Avery 2007, 41–61.

Wenger, Beth S. *The Jewish Americans: Three Centuries of Jewish Voices in America*. New York: Doubleday, 2007.

"Where Life Is All Drama." *The Rochester Democrat and Chronicle*. Aug. 29, 1926. www.fultonhistory.com. Accessed June 24, 2012.

Whitfield, Stephen. *In Search of American Jewish Culture*. Waltham: Brandeis UP, 1999.

Wilson, Christopher P. *White Collar Fictions: Class and Social Representation in American Literature, 1885–1925*. Athens: U of Georgia P, 1992.

Wilson, Mollie. "So Big." www.tabletmag.com/arts-and-culture/books/819/so-big/. May 2, 2007. Accessed June 24, 2012.

Wollstein, R. Heylbut. "Girls—Seen By Edna Ferber." *New York Times*. May 11, 1924. 12.

Wren, Celia. "A Musical Revival Navigates New Currents." *Washington Post*. Nov. 8, 2009. E4.

Yardley, Jonathan. "Ferber's 'Giant,' Cut Down to Size." *Washington Post*. May 8, 2006. C1.

Index